The Strange Silence of the Bible in the Church

BOOKS BY JAMES D. SMART
Published by The Westminster Press

The Cultural Subversion of the Biblical Faith:
  Life in the 20th Century Under the Sign of the Cross

Doorway to a New Age:
  A Study of Paul's Letter to the Romans

The Strange Silence of the Bible in the Church:
  A Study in Hermeneutics

The Quiet Revolution:
  The Radical Impact of Jesus on Men of His Time

The ABC's of Christian Faith

The Divided Mind of Modern Theology:
  Karl Barth and Rudolf Bultmann, 1908–1933

History and Theology in Second Isaiah:
  A Commentary on Isaiah 35, 40–66

The Old Testament in Dialogue with Modern Man

The Creed in Christian Teaching

The Interpretation of Scripture

Servants of the Word: The Prophets of Israel
  (Westminster Guides to the Bible)

The Rebirth of Ministry

The Teaching Ministry of the Church

The Recovery of Humanity

What a Man Can Believe

A Promise to Keep

Jesus, Stories for Children

In Collaboration with David Noel Freedman

God Has Spoken

The Strange Silence of the Bible in the Church

A STUDY IN HERMENEUTICS

by
James D. Smart

THE WESTMINSTER PRESS
Philadelphia

ISBN 0-664-24894-2

LIBRARY OF CONGRESS CATALOG CARD No. 72-118323

BOOK DESIGN BY
DOROTHY ALDEN SMITH

Published by The Westminster Press ®
Philadelphia, Pennsylvania

PRINTED IN THE UNITED STATES OF AMERICA

6   7   8   9   10

Contents

Preface

SEVERAL years ago a young man, about thirty-five years of age, told me a curious story. He had not been inside a church in more than twenty years. He had knocked about the world, had been married and divorced, had become reasonably successful in business, and recently, because of a sense of emptiness in his life, had begun to read the Bible. But the Bible frustrated him. It suggested meanings and then entangled them in problems that were for him impenetrable. He visited several churches, not on Sunday but on weekdays, to inquire about the availability of instruction in the Bible, but at each of them he found himself regarded as somewhat of a freak. Phone calls to other churches produced only embarrassment. Finally, one day coming upon a display of Bibles in a store window and seeing the sign "Bible Society," he entered and inquired of a clerk where he could study the Bible. She asked him to come back the next day for an answer and, when he returned, sent him to the five-session Lenten lecture series of a large city church. The church, however, offered adults no other opportunity for study of the Bible!

It was, perhaps, that story which started me investigating what has been happening to the Bible in the church, and the fruit of the investigation is this book. My finding is that the Bible is in a very bad way in the church. In a century during which Biblical scholarship has made tremendous

advances in America, with literature on the Bible expanding enormously and a number of new highly readable
translations becoming "best sellers," there has been an
increasing frustration of preachers with the Scriptures as a
basis for sermons, a steady decline in the educational use of
the Bible in the church, and a mounting ignorance of the
contents of the Bible among members of the church. It is a
puzzling phenomenon. I am convinced that it constitutes the
crisis beneath all the other crises that endanger the church's
future. The church that no longer hears the essential message of the Scriptures soon ceases to understand what it is
for and is open to be captured by the dominant religious
philosophy of the moment, which is usually some blend of
cultural nationalism with Christianity. All distinctions become blurred when the voices of the original prophets and
apostles are stilled.

Responsibility for this strange silence of the Bible in the
church does not rest upon preachers alone. Much too often
they have borne the whole reproach without there being
any recognition of the complex character of the dilemma in
which they find themselves. Rather, there has been a blindness which scholar, preacher, teacher, and layman, all alike,
have shared—a blindness to the complexity of the essential
hermeneutical problem, which, in simple terms, is the problem of how to translate the full content of an ancient text
into the language and life-context of late twentieth-century
persons. Reproaches should be kept to a minimum and the
attention concentrated upon getting to the roots of a situation
in which we are all involved. Our futures and the future of
the church depend upon the finding of a viable solution.
This book does not profess to offer that solution, ready-made.
The dimensions of the problem are of a magnitude that forbids any such presumption. The present study claims only to
disclose the nature of the problem and to point in the direction in which the solution is likely to be found if we are
willing to devote our energies to the finding of it in the years
ahead.

The major substance of these chapters was delivered in four lectures at two theological seminaries; in October, 1968, at Columbia Seminary in Decatur, Georgia, and in January, 1969, at Midwestern Baptist Seminary in Kansas City, Missouri. I was encouraged to enlarge the lectures into a book by the warm interest shown by the members of the faculty in both institutions and I take this occasion to express my gratitude to them for the generosity of their reception. I must also thank my colleagues, George M. Landes and Edmund A. Steimle, for their kindness in reading the manuscript and making suggestions for its improvement.

J.D.S.

Union Theological Seminary

The Strange Silence of the Bible
in the Church

I

The Growing Silence
of the Scriptures

PROTESTANTISM has long prided itself upon the attention
that it gives to the Bible. Conservative churchmen have
exalted it so unquestioningly that their attitude verges upon
idolatry. Liberal churchmen have insisted that the questions
which the Biblical text raises for a well-informed twentieth-
century mind must be faced with honesty but rarely have
they shown any inclination to remove the Bible from its
central place in the worship of the Christian congregation
or in the educational program of the church school. Any
open attack upon the Bible as a whole, or even upon the
Old Testament portion of it, or any attempt to reduce it to a
subordinate status in the church, would undoubtedly meet
with almost universal resistance. But let the deed be done
unobtrusively, not by any concerted plan of any faction but
as the result of factors that are at work unconsciously in all
of us, and let the surface appearance be maintained so that
what has been happening below the surface escapes the
notice of most people, and we could awaken one day to find
ourselves a church almost totally alienated from the Scriptures.

If that is a description of our present situation, and I
am convinced that it is, then surely it is permissible to sound
an alarm. The voice of the Scriptures is falling silent in the
preaching and teaching of the church and in the consciousness of Christian people, a silence that is perceptible even

among those who are most insistent upon their devotion to the Scriptures. To this must be added a second statement that will sound equally outrageous, that this falling silent of the Scriptures is at least in some degree, directly or indirectly, a consequence of what has been happening in Biblical scholarship in this century. The first statement sounds like the complaint of a jaundiced mind that is always seeing its own day as a decline from some brighter, better, earlier day. The second sounds suspiciously like what fundamentalists have long been claiming in their condemnation of historical-critical scholarship. Let it be plain, then, that no idealization of an earlier era is intended, no questioning of the basic principles of historical criticism, and no such ignorant assumption as that a church innocent of critical scholarship reads the Bible with greater profit because of that innocence.

It can hardly be questioned that, in wide sections of the North American church, people today are not as frequently exposed to the Scriptures as they were in the precritical era. Preachers who were untroubled by historical and literary analysis were much freer in their use of Scripture. The Bible was read with greater intensity when there was an expectation that suddenly in any sentence from Genesis to Revelation there might be a message from God himself. Adult and youth classes that met regularly for the study of the Bible have now vanished in many congregations and, where the classes still meet, they give their attention usually to matters that seem to them more urgent than the understanding of Scripture. Midweek meetings for Bible study are largely a thing of the past and so also is the second service on Sunday, which gave the preacher an opportunity to approach the Bible more thoroughly with at least a segment of his congregation. The final stage in this reduction of time spent with the Bible is the shortening of the Sunday morning sermon, which for most church members has been their one remaining possibility of contact with the Bible. That people were more frequently exposed to the Bible does not necessarily mean that its intrinsic message was heard more clearly, was understood more deeply, or was appropriated more richly. One can easily find churches where constant attention is given to Scripture which seem to be totally devoid of any Biblical insight on questions such as race, nation, wealth, war, ecumenical relations between Christian churches, and the total responsibility of the church for the world beyond itself. Nevertheless it is striking that in the years during which Biblical interpretation has become ever more complex, requiring more time and concentrated attention if one is to profit from it, the church's life has fallen into a pattern that provides a diminishing amount of time for the study of Scripture.

Why are church members less eager for exposure to the Bible and why are ministers less eager to expose them to it? It is obvious and incontestable that the preparation of a sermon on a Biblical text is much more difficult than it was in precritical days. Most ministers have been made aware in seminary how easily Scripture may be misinterpreted. Getting at the original meaning of a text is a fairly complicated process if it is done properly and it requires concentrated study. Then the preacher may also be aware of a possible clash between the sophistication of a scholarly approach and the naïveté of some of his more literal-minded members. Why risk a possible misunderstanding when in the few minutes that are available there is so much that needs urgently to be said to people burdened with the desperate issues of personal and social life in the modern age? We can see here a superficial effect of the increased complexity of Biblical interpretation, but the question remains how it is possible in a church that still acknowledges its dependence upon the Scriptures for them to be so easily pushed to one side. The church in its practice seems to be going in a direction opposite to what is demanded of it by the development in Biblical scholarship and by its own avowed principles. The natural expectation has been that with the advance of scholarship there would be a widening and deepening of modern man's understanding of the message of Scripture. But, strangely, the steady progress of scholarship, constantly perfecting its methodology for dealing with the problems that the text of Scripture provides for it, has been paralleled by this equally steady recession in the attention that the church and Christians give to the Bible.

The progress of Biblical scholarship in this century has been impressive. The history that forms the background of both Testaments has been reconstructed from fragments distilled from the records or unearthed by archaeologists. The traditions embodied in the documents have been disentangled and each placed in its own historical setting. The religious ideas and practices of each period have been illuminated by the contemporary phenomena in the surrounding Near Eastern world. By means of form and tradition criticism we have been able to probe behind the written records and trace the process by which each tradition has come into its present form. Comparative linguistics with ever more accurate definition of the changes in the meaning of words in different periods has brought us closer to each author's original intention. A sharpening of theological interest has taken us more deeply into his mind. And an increased sensitivity to the theological accent of each of the authors has greatly broadened our appreciation of the variety of voices that make up the choir of Scripture. Also, it must be recognized that these investigations have not been allowed to remain hidden in volumes accessible only to specially trained scholars. There is an immense literature now at the disposal of the nonspecialist for the understanding and interpretation of Scripture. And yet the embarrassment of every educational program in churches large and small is the difficulty in finding persons who understand the Scriptures sufficiently to be able to interpret them intelligently to anyone else. Neither their years in church school nor their years of listening to sermons has taken them far enough into the Scriptures for them to find their way about by themselves or for their daily life to be guided and sustained by what they hear. The diminishing of opportunity for exposure to Scripture which we have observed would lead us to expect in the immediate future not an improvement but an accentuation of this situation.

We are likely to be most aware of this recession of the Bible in the church's interest at the point of the Old Testament. And here a relation between the advance of scholarship and the decline of interest can be most easily established. The nineteenth century in Germany laid the foundations of the whole modern approach to the investigation of Scripture. Not until the fourth quarter of the century and the beginning of the twentieth century did it begin to spill over effectively into our English-speaking world. The achievements of scholars such as Herder, Eichhorn, De Wette, Vatke, Wellhausen, and Gunkel were monumental. No one can question that as a consequence of their work the Old Testament was vastly more comprehensible at the end of the century than it was at the beginning, and, compared with the two previous centuries, the difference was like that between light and darkness. Yet the theologians who dominated that century in Germany and shaped the minds of Christians are distinguished by a distaste for the Old Testament. Schleiermacher would have preferred to have it as an appendix to the New Testament. Hegel and Ritschl had little interest in it. Harnack, while he thought Marcion wrong in excluding it from the Christian canon in the second century, was convinced that the church would be better without it in the modern age. By 1900 the Old Testament had in general been reduced to the status of historical background for the understanding of the New Testament, a standpoint that has been carried forward and given new prestige in the present era by Rudolf Bultmann and some of his disciples. One can imagine what effect this has had on the use of the Old Testament in the church. To deny it canonicity[1] is to deny the validity of using it as a basis for Christian preaching.

Not until the third decade in the present century did Old Testament scholars in Germany begin to recognize that a serious defect in their hermeneutic was responsible for this disparagement of the Old Testament and its growing disuse in the church. Their perfectly valid investigation of the literature, history, and religion of Israel had tended to remove the Old Testament into a distant, alien world that was left behind when the Christian gospel burst upon mankind, a world fascinating in its interest for the scholar but so far below the Christian level at many points that it was feared the use of its Scriptures by the church might generate a sub-Christian mentality. The differences between the Old and the New Testament were so accentuated that the unity of the Testaments was almost completely lost from sight. Since 1920 German Old Testament scholars, and many beyond Germany, have worked valiantly to remedy the situation. The proposal of Nazi Christians to remove the Old Testament from the Bible undoubtedly spurred and lent passion to the consideration of what validates the presence of Israel's Scriptures in the Christian Bible. The theological unity of the Testaments has been explored as never before. The validity of Christian preaching from the Old Testament has been vindicated with great thoroughness. But, if we may trust the observation of Walther Zimmerli, an eminent German Old Testament scholar, neither the church nor the systematic theologian who explicates its faith have as yet been much influenced by the new development in interpretation. In his Sprunt Lectures of 1963 he says: "The Old Testament is an alien factor in recent Protestant theology. . . . The Old Testament is honored and its words are read from the pulpit, yet when the systematic theologian endeavors to unfold what the Christian faith is, and to describe it in its essential parts, then the Old Testament is chiefly an embarrassment. . . . The situation can arise in which a hermeneutic which attempts seriously to grasp the real content of the New Testament proclamation no longer sees a need for the word and proclamation of the Old." [2] What happened in the German church has had its parallel in America, but because the disappearance of the Old Testament from the preaching, and even from the Scripture readings in many churches, has taken place so quietly, without anyone's calling attention to it either in advocacy or in criticism, we may be blind to the fact that it has happened.

In all the discussion of the Old Testament and concern about its abandonment, the assumption has tended to be made that it is only the Old Testament that has been allowed to fall silent in the church, that there is no serious problem about the New Testament. Whatever may have happened to the Old Testament, we tell ourselves we are still safe to this degree, that the New Testament retains its voice among Christian people. But this is essentially an illusion. We should be warned by what happened in the second century when Marcion's crude silencing of the Old Testament was combined with a more subtle silencing of the New Testament by the reading of a Hellenistic gospel into its text. And we should be warned by what happened a few years ago in Germany when a Nazi abandonment of the Old Testament was combined with an exceedingly subtle reading of a nationalistic gospel into the New Testament.[3] The Testaments seem to have a way of preserving their own unity and to live or die together. The basic problem is not just the silence of the Old Testament in the church but rather the silence of the Scriptures as a whole. The complaint of theological students, which may be taken as symptomatic of a much larger constituency, is not that they find the Old Testament irrelevant but that the language and thought forms of Scripture as a whole are alien to them—often they find the New Testament thought forms the more alien and the Old Testament with its down-to-earth practicality the more relevant. All of us to some degree share the illusion that it is easier, less problematical, to deal with a New Testament text. The illusion is created by the greater familiarity. But, if the intention is to let the text come to expression with its own original significance, the familiar text has to recover its strangeness and disentangle itself from the religious and ethical meanings that we so readily place upon it. The very familiarity of the words conceals the strangeness and distinctiveness of the meaning, which does not disclose itself to hasty and superficial investigation.

We traced earlier a narrowing in the exposure of Christians to Scripture. We have now to show that at the points of continued exposure the channel of communication is narrowed still further. The Bible is not ignored. Most preachers are actuated by an earnest concern to bring the message of the Scriptures to bear upon the problems of their people. But the topical form of sermon, which seems to have the widest appeal today, both to preachers and to people, usually permits the Biblical text to be touched only lightly. There is not room in it for any very careful exposition. Undoubtedly this preference for the topical sermon is a reaction from an earlier form of expository preaching that became deadly in its dullness. A topical discussion can more easily be kept relevant to the immediate concerns of the listeners. But it inhibits the function of the sermon as a channel between the Scriptures and the church of today. Sermons are rarely heard which open the Scriptures to the community in such a way that the people themselves begin to be able to find their way back and forth between their life situation and the resources to illuminate their life situation that are available to them in the Scriptures. It is only our ineptitude that makes words dull which in their original utterance shook the community that heard them to the depths and endangered the lives of the speakers. Sermons should be doorways through which the men and women of the Bible find their way into our world and we into their world until in converse with them we become one unbroken fellowship that bridges the centuries. The typical sermon of today offers little opportunity for the kind of reeducation in the understanding of Scripture which is necessary if the church is to recapture that kind of continuity with its origins.

We might consider also what happens to the Bible in the private practices of Christians. An astounding number of Bibles are purchased each year, more than eight million in the United States alone. Each new translation becomes a best seller. What people do with these Bibles remains a mystery. If they read them, it is likely to be at bed time, just a few verses until one comes upon a helpful thought. The practice is generally regarded as praiseworthy, one of the last surviving bastions of a true piety. But, in spite of what it may have meant as inspiration to countless individuals, it may have to be reckoned as a hindrance to the understanding of the Bible in the church. It has tended to make the Bible primarily a book for use in private devotions. But the Bible was not written to be used in that way and certainly not to be read in snippets of five or six verses each. No part of it (with the exception perhaps of a few psalms) in its origin was intended for private consumption. It is distinctively a public book. The prophets brought their *nation* before God. The Pentateuch and the Deuteronomic history represent the attempt of a *community*, a people of God, to grasp what God had been doing with them in their past that they might see more clearly their way as a people into the future. The psalms are the prayers and praises of the whole *community* of Israel. The Gospels are the *church's* remembrance of the words and events that called them into existence as a new people of God, a new Israel, and committed them to a redemptive mission in history. Paul's major letters are all of them to *churches* and lose much of their force unless they are heard as apostolic instruction in what it means to be a *church*. The Bible is marching orders for an army, not bedtime reading to help one sleep more soundly.

The Bible is a book to be studied by the Christian community. Make it primarily devotional literature for private use and no longer is it given the attention it requires but, more seriously still, it is subjected to an intensely individualistic interpretation and thereby silenced at the most incisive points of its message.

It is difficult for Protestants to credit this alleged silencing of the Bible in their midst. The Bible is still there in solitary grandeur on their pulpit, or at least on the reading desk. Honor is constantly paid to it. Everyone treats it with respect. Even a person who has not looked inside it since childhood would hesitate to destroy even a thoroughly dilapidated copy. Lessons are read from it in every service of worship. References are made to it in sermons. The curriculum of the church school gives it a prominent place. Has not the quality of Biblical teaching in our theological seminaries improved tremendously in the past fifty years? Also, in many of our colleges and universities there are courses in Bible open to undergraduates that are both high in quality and popular with the students. Resistance to critical scholarship, which was intense fifty years ago, in most of the major denominations has now vanished almost completely and is found only in the ultraconservative fringe. But test the graduates of our church schools, or the candidates for the ministry who appear each year at the doors of our seminaries, or the office-bearers who determine the policies of our churches, concerning their knowledge and understanding of the Scriptures, and one is stabbed awake to the fact that something is seriously wrong.

The seriousness of the situation is that the fading of the Scriptures from the consciousness of the church weakens and then ruptures the continuity of the church of today with the church in which it had its origin, so that it no longer remembers the word that called it into being or the purpose that alone justifies its existence. There is no stronger evidence of the subtle forces in life that resist God than the speed with which a church that no longer hears the Scriptures finds itself transferred from the service of God to the service of itself and its members, turned inward upon itself rather than outward toward the world. We call the church the body of Christ, but it remains his body only insofar as it is open, responsive, and obedient to his mind and spirit as they confront us ever afresh in the witness of Scripture. Let the Scriptures cease to be heard and soon the remembered Christ becomes an imagined Christ, shaped by the religiosity and the unconscious desires of his worshipers. Every renewal of the church in history has been a consequence of men, after a time of deafness, recovering the ears with which to hear not just the words but the strange, disturbing, yet gracious, word that is somehow hidden in the words until it meets the hearer who is ready for it.

Protestants have rejoiced at what they have seen happening in the Catholic Church in recent years. For centuries, in reaction to the Protestant polemics based on the Bible, the Catholic Church withheld the Scriptures from its people, gave them little prominence in its preaching and discouraged the introduction of modern historical-critical scholarship. But in 1943 the papal encyclical *Divino afflante Spiritu* gave Catholic scholars their freedom to use all the tools of modern research in their investigation and interpretation of Scripture. New translations were sponsored, new commentaries projected, and Catholic people in many lands began an exciting adventure into the Bible. The fruits of that development are all about us. Barriers have melted. Structures that held the church imprisoned for centuries have begun to change. The achievements of Pope John XXIII and Vatican Council were possible only through the liberating authority of a rediscovered gospel. Those who in high places have now become frightened by the changes that are taking place and try to halt them do not reckon with the nature and dimensions of the power that is at work behind the changes. They have let the Scriptures loose in their church and they must accept the consequences.

But do Protestants who observe this ferment with such satisfaction note the absence of any such excitement about the Scriptures in our Protestant churches? We have our own paralysis of religious structures, naturally in a variety of forms in our pluralistic order and enforced from below by the will of the many rather than from above by the will of an autocratic curia. Because these structures take on the authority of a religious tradition they become difficult to change and a younger generation, demanding change, is tempted to despair. But we should know that it takes a word that has in it the authority of God himself to expose the relativity of all human words and practices and to keep us as a Christian community from becoming the prisoners of our traditions. There is an intimate relation between the paralysis of structures that we lament and the fading of the voice of Scripture in the ears of our people. The secret of Israel's pilgrimage forward through the centuries was the word from which the prophets would not let them get free, that had in it both God's judgment upon their present state and his promise for their future. Incarnate in Jesus and his gospel the same word has again and again had to blast the church loose from its static formulations and set it in movement toward its goal. How that word is to find its freedom in the church today is our concern. If it is to reach the world, it must have other channels made for it than just the Sunday sermon.

Responsibility for the situation in Protestantism that we have described may be placed in various quarters. No single factor explains it. From one angle it is a consequence of modern education that inevitably generates embarrassing questions about the Scriptures even for a ten-year-old child, questions that frequently receive no answers either in church or in church school. The impression easily gets abroad that the Bible contains a body of antiquated knowledge that no longer claims our serious attention. Certainly, too, the spirit of the age is unfriendly to the idea that delving into ancient documents may produce the wisdom that is needed by our scientific and technological culture. Again, one may point to an educational structure in the church, so flimsy and brief, yet loaded with such extensive tasks that even at its best it merely pricks the surface of the Scriptures. The preacher complains that, as Biblical research increases in complexity, careful exegesis of his own becomes a forbidding and time-consuming task in his busy schedule, and the Biblical scholar who trained him attributes the preacher's failure to use the excellent equipment with which the seminary has provided him either to an intellectual laziness or, more charitably, to the intolerable pressures of the modern American pastorate. The fundamentalist blames it all on the "higher critics," who, he says, have torn the Bible to pieces and destroyed men's respect for it as the word of God. And the higher critic blames the fundamentalist, who has insisted that Christians read the Bible with an unquestioning naïveté that has been abandoned in every other realm of life, a sacrifice of mental integrity that few persons are any longer prepared to make. But all these alleged influences have been at best secondary factors in what has happened. The primary source of the Bible's failure to maintain its place in the life of the church and in the lives of Christian people is a multiple breakdown in communication: between Biblical scholars and those responsible for preaching and teaching, between preachers and people, and, not least, between the separate departments into which the faculty of a theological seminary is divided.

the most important issue raised in this chapter is: how do we get from what the text meant to what the text means.

II

Hermeneutics
and Homiletics

THE MAN who feels most painfully the church's embarrassment and frustration with the Scriptures is the preacher. There may here and there be preachers so enamored with their modern enlightenment and so confident that they have left their Palestinian origins far behind that they see no reason to focus the church's attention so exclusively upon the Bible but rather are inclined to find their inspiration in literature less remote in time. But they are a small minority. The vast majority of preachers are bound to the Scriptures, perhaps by the tradition in which they stand with varying degrees of willingness, perhaps by their personal conviction and most earnest desire to be interpreters of the message of the Scriptures to their people. Week by week they stand between these ancient records of faith and the complex situations of a modern community, and, more often than they would like to admit, they themselves are conscious that it is something less than the judgment and mercy, the promise and hope and joy, that are embodied in the Scriptures that they have communicated to their people. When they open the Bible they are overwhelmed by the complexity of the problems with which the text confronts them, problems first of their own understanding and then the even more difficult ones of how to interpret the Biblical text to the man in the pew and the man in the street.

the preacher

Many preachers today feel themselves trapped and imprisoned in an intolerable situation in regard to the Bible. They are bound by their vows and their tradition to a book that is more of a burden to them than an infinite resource. Not more than 5 percent of it has been useful to them in their preaching and teaching. And yet they are expected to preach from it and to teach it incessantly. In seminary their training in exegesis was concentrated upon textual, literary, and historical problems. They learned to place the text in its original historical situation and to hear it with the accents of the ancient speaker or author. They had a general introduction to each of the Testaments as a whole. They were made familiar with the vast variety of problems with which the Scriptures confront the scholar and the even vaster variety of solutions to those problems which across the years have been devised by the scholars. But at two points they are unlikely to remember much in their seminary training that is a help to them: on how to get from the original meaning of a text in its ancient situation to the meaning of the same text in a late twentieth-century world, or on how to deal honestly and adequately with the critical problems generated by the Biblical text when they confront the rudimentary educational milieu of a local congregation.

The predicament of the preacher has been created to a large extent by the hiatus between the Biblical and the practical departments in our theological seminaries. We are victims of specialization. It can happen that even the two sections of the Biblical department, Old and New Testament specialists, go their separate ways for years without any discussion of their common concerns as expositors of a Christian Bible. And much more easily it happens that those who are engaged in the complex tasks of Biblical interpretation become isolated from those whose function it is to train future ministers in preaching and teaching. Hermeneutics is developed in one compartment while homiletics and Christian education go their way separately. What adds to the problem, as we shall see more clearly later, is that not all Biblical scholars are interested in the full task of hermeneutics. "Hermeneutics" is a comprehensive term that embraces all the elements that enter into the interpretation of Scripture—linguistics, textual criticism, literary analysis, form and tradition criticism, historical exegesis, and theological exposition—and its full task is to move from a determination of the original meaning of a text to a translation of that meaning into contemporary language and thought forms. In some quarters the function of Biblical scholarship is limited to the determination of the original meaning and the student is left to discover the seriousness of the full hermeneutical problem when first he takes his place as an interpreter between the Scriptures and the community that is represented by his congregation.

Homiletics has far too often been considered merely practical training in the construction and delivery of sermons rather than a seriously theological discipline that focuses its critical attention upon how the whole theological enterprise and the whole life of the church comes to expression in preaching. Insofar as preaching is regarded as bound to the Scriptures, homiletics has as its task the training of men to translate the evangelical content of the Scriptures into sermons that will let the voices of prophets and apostles continue to be heard in a contemporary form. At once it is evident that hermeneutics and homiletics have much in common. They are focused both of them on the same problem but at different levels. And yet, in our English-speaking world the two have not had much serious conversation with each other but have gone their ways each of them in almost total isolation from the other. The Biblical scholar has tended to confine himself to the purely descriptive task of defining what the Biblical text originally meant, a sufficiently complex task now to engage all his attention, with only an occasional aside concerning contemporary meanings. Rarely has he ventured out on the journey from then to now that constitutes the task of hermeneutics. The homiletician may from time to time teach a class jointly with an Old or New Testament scholar in order to link more closely the concerns of exegesis and sermon construction and to probe cautiously into the area of hermeneutics. But rarely has anyone attempted to look at the total problem of the relation between what has been happening in the whole range of Biblical interpretation and what is happening now in the exposition of the Bible in the preaching and teaching of the church.

It is high time that all of us—scholars, preachers, and laymen—took a long, hard look at the existing situation. We have perhaps assumed that every advance in the realm of Biblical scholarship must issue in a more enlightened use of the Bible in the church and a greater availability of the Bible's resources of wisdom and spiritual power for modern man. But what meets our eyes is the puzzling and embarrassing phenomenon that the century in which the investigation of the Bible has been prosecuted most scientifically, most vigorously, and with an international cooperation of scholars, has witnessed a steady recession of the Bible from the preaching of the church and from the consciousness of Christian people. This is not what we expected. It is most unreasonable that it should be so. Therefore, as reasonable men we have closed our eyes to the facts until the facts have come to constitute a crisis for the Bible in the church.

The present study could therefore be described as an attempt to bring two isolated disciplines of theology, whose cooperation with each other is essential to the church's health, into vital conversation with each other. Because of their separation a breakdown in communication has taken place. The knowledge that is available in the realm of scholarship for the understanding and interpretation of the Bible has somehow failed to flow out through the church's preaching and teaching into the minds and lives of the people. As a consequence the church is threatened with a disaster that can only be likened to a man going blind. John Calvin expressed a profound truth when he called the Scriptures the spectacles that correct the astigmatism occasioned by man's sin and enable him to see himself, his fellowman, and his world as they really are, all of them in the light of God's presence. Prophets, psalmists, historians, apostles, with Jesus Christ at their center, lend us their eyes through the medium of Scripture. Take away the Scriptures, and the church, with all its members, begins to go blind, so that it becomes incapable of being redemptive salt in the contemporary world. The disaster spreads from the church to the community for which the church is responsible and which it exists to serve. The dimensions of the problem are immense and its complexity is forbidding. The most one can expect to do in a small book is to get the subject open for investigation.

If the discussion has a somewhat belligerent tone at times, it is because of the magnitude of the obstacles in the way. There are deeply entrenched attitudes among both scholars and preachers that must be confronted and overcome if we are to achieve a solution to the church's problem. To be scientific should mean to be open to new aspects of a subject and new forms of investigation, yet sometimes among scholars an established methodology takes on all the characteristics of a rigid orthodoxy. So also some one form of preaching, in one area the topical, in another the evangelistic, may become so strong a tradition that only the boldest dare to diverge from it. We fool ourselves if we think that such orthodoxies are to be shaken and displaced without a struggle.

The intimate relation between hermeneutics and homiletics should be evident, then, to everyone who is concerned for the continuity of the present-day church with the community of faith in which it had its origin and which is documented for us in the Scriptures as a whole. Hermeneutics engages in an investigation of how Scripture has been interpreted in the past and is being interpreted today in order to discover the method of interpretation that is most appropriate to and consonant with its total content and its ultimate meaning for man. That content and meaning have as their primary channel of communication to the ordinary man, and for most members of the church the only channel, the preaching that takes place in Sunday worship. Homiletics, on the other hand, submits the church's preaching constantly to critical scrutiny in order to free it from its perversions and to enable it to find the form in which the gospel will come most clearly and forcefully to expression. But the preacher has no access to a really Christian gospel except through the Scriptures. And how the Scriptures are interpreted determines in a very large measure the character of the gospel that is preached. The preacher is dependent on the scholarly interpreter. But what is equally true but much less frequently recognized is that there are depths of meaning in the text of Scripture which remain hidden from the scholar until the text is preached.[4] The ultimate content of Scripture is a word in which God comes to man in judgment and in mercy, which has to be proclaimed and heard and have its fruits in life before anyone, even though he be the most accomplished scholar, can rightly understand its nature. The criterion by which the scholar must evaluate his hermeneutic is defective, therefore, until the question is faced what effect it has upon the hearing of that vital word in the church. Biblical scholars and preachers are partners in a common venture, dependent upon each other, and the work of each is likely to be futile without the other.

This becomes even clearer when we see that each on his own level is faced with the task of making the journey successfully from the original meaning of the Biblical text in its historical situation to the contemporary meaning of the same text in the immediate situation of the present-day world. The preacher faces each week the problem of bringing together the world that meets him in the Bible and the world in which he is living, of finding his way from an ancient text to a restatement of the meaning of that text in terms that will make sense and have significance for his congregation and community. He has to venture out each time afresh on a perilous road from then to now, perilous because there are so many ways in which he can lose the essential content of his text (or can lose his listeners) in the course of the journey. The broad gap between then and now is the region in which so many students and preachers get lost. Their training in seminary was much more concentrated on the "then" than on how to get from then to now. The Biblical departments in seminary rightly make the student labor with care to discern what the text meant when it was first written or spoken. But frequently the assumption is made that, without any further research or assistance or extension of his methodology, he can move from the original meaning to the contemporary meaning, as though there were no serious problems in making that transition. Anyone who has had to travel that road week by week knows differently and has experienced the depth of the problem. And perhaps to his surprise he has found that the more thorough his grounding in a scientific historical exegesis the wider the gap seems to become and the greater the difficulty in moving with integrity from the original meaning to the expression of that meaning without loss or perversion in preaching and teaching today.

But hermeneutics is the study of how all the resources of Biblical and theological scholarship may be mobilized to accompany the preacher on his journey. It seeks to lay open the nature of the problems he faces, problems of language and thought forms, problems of historical understanding, theological problems, which, unresolved, become insuperable obstacles to the completion of the journey. It challenges the complacency of a scholarship that thinks it has finished its task when it has equipped the student to get at the "then" of his text accurately and sends him out to make the whole journey from "then" to "now" with no other resources. It challenges also the assumption that the original meaning can be understood in isolation from the present meaning. Hermeneutics should therefore be the scholarly companion not only of the preacher and the teacher but also of the layman whose assimilation of the preaching and teaching alone renders them effective. At first hermeneutics may seem to complicate the understanding of Scripture, making intricate what formerly seemed simple, invoking mysteries where formerly all was rational and plain, and exposing a variety of problems and pitfalls that were unnoticed before. But, like any science, it has as one of its functions the clearing away of illusions and the disclosure of the realities of our situation, enabling us to see with a new clarity the shape of the problems with which we have to deal.

Hermeneutics has not always been a neglected discipline. In the nineteenth century when Biblical scholarship in Europe was struggling with problems of methodology, significant works appeared.[5] And in the last decades of the nineteenth century and the first of the twentieth, when in the English-speaking world a historical-critical methodology was making its revolutionary impact upon the mind of the church, book after book appeared with the purpose of showing how the new approach, far from being destructive, actually enabled the text of Scripture to speak with a much greater meaningfulness.[6] But there was an excess of confidence that the new methodology had solved the problem of interpretation once and for all.[7] Minor changes would still be made, but essentially there was no longer any need for hermeneutical investigation! The whole history of interpretation was portrayed as a progress, at first very slow, then in the final century very rapid, leading up to the perfected science of the present. That confidence in some quarters still persists. And where it persists there is a decided hostility to the reopening of the hermeneutic question. But it *has* been reopened by some of the ablest of our twentieth-century Biblical scholars and theologians and one of the significant features of the discussion during the past fifty years has been the way in which, wherever it has exerted its influence, it has stimulated the interest of Old and New Testament scholars in the issue of their scholarship in preaching.[8] The intimate relation between historical exegesis and the exposition of Scripture in the life of the church has commanded an increasing attention. But in our English-speaking world the old isolation has tended to persist, partly because in an era of specialization we have permitted the different departments of theology to proceed in almost complete independence of each other, partly because of a tendency of theology to see itself as a scientific academic discipline rather than as a critical function of the church, but most of all because we have merely continued a highly respected established order without asking what it is doing to the church and to man in our time.

Hermeneutics serves as a link between all the theological disciplines since at some point it draws each of them into participation in its concerns. In a Protestant seminary it is taken for granted that hermeneutics belongs in the Biblical department, but in a Catholic seminary it is likely to be placed in the department of dogmatics since it not only involves a doctrine of Scripture but probes into the underlying theological assumptions of the interpreter. Again, since the history of interpretation is an essential aspect of hermeneutics, it could in part belong in the department of history. Gerhard Ebeling in an extended essay defends the thesis that the whole history of the church is an unfolding of the content of Scripture, and therefore can be understood as a continuous exercise in hermeneutics.[9] And with its interest in how interpretation finally issues in preaching and teaching, hermeneutics reaches into the departments of homiletics and Christian education. Because of this wide-ranging involvement it serves to break down the walls between the theological disciplines, exposing their interdependence and drawing them into closer cooperation with eath other.

It is necessary perhaps to point out that there is an "s" on the end of the word "hermeneutics." One of our more recent theological movements has chosen to call itself the "New Hermeneutic" and its adherents take great pains to establish a distinction between "hermeneutic" and "hermeneutics." Whereas hermeneutics, like exegesis, dogmatics, and homiletics, is a basic theological discipline that engages the interest of scholars with widely varying theological orientations, the "New Hermeneutic" claims to be nothing less than the theological wave of the future. As one proponent expresses it, first there was Ritschlianism, then Barthianism, and now the New Hermeneutic.[10] Two distinctive characteristics of the movement which certainly would be alien to a basic discipline of hermeneutics are an attempt to harness the existentialist philosophy of Martin Heidegger to the tasks of Biblical interpretation and a resolute ignoring of the continued presence of the Old Testament in the canon of Scripture. What the movement will achieve has yet to be seen. Certainly, scholars such as Gerhard Ebeling, Ernst Fuchs, and James Robinson have opened up important veins of research and have demonstrated both the urgency and the complexity of the problems of interpretation. Whatever may be the value of the "New Hermeneutic," they have made important contributions to hermeneutics. Their existentialist assumptions and language has tended at times to foster a high degree of obscurity in their writings, creating the impression of an esoteric circle that one cannot enter or understand until he has committed himself unreservedly to the principles and language of the circle. Undoubtedly this has had the effect of making hermeneutics seem a more difficult and mystifying subject than it is. But the most unfortunate aspect of the adoption of "hermeneutic" in the title of a distinctive theological movement is that it is likely to conceal from many people the fact that hermeneutics is a basic concern of all of us who are interested in letting the message of the Scriptures be heard in our time, no matter what particular theology has thus far commanded our allegiance.[11] It would be as reasonable to label a new movement in theology the "New Dogmatic" or even the "New Homiletic" as the "New Hermeneutic." Neither dogmatics, nor homiletics, nor hermeneutics can be made the monoply of any one group of theologians. Both terms, hermeneutic and hermeneutics, may be used with no greater distinction being intended than that the singular form denotes the interpretative approach of some one man or school while the plural signifies the total discipline with its wide variety of approaches.

III

The Reopening
of the Hermeneutical Question

ONE CAN UNDERSTAND the reluctance of many Biblical scholars to take account of the effect of their researches upon the use of the Bible in the church. From its very beginning the application of a scientific methodology to the study of the Scriptures has scandalized a wide section of the church. Traditional interpretations of a book that for centuries has been venerated as sacrosanct, in each word the medium of divine revelation, die hard, and the procurement of their death has seemed to many to be a blasphemous mutilation of the sacred book. Therefore scholars have long been accustomed to attacks on their methodology and have had to be on their guard against pressures from the church to soften the impact of critical research. The pressures at an early stage were crude and brutal resulting in the dismissal of scholars from their posts. With the general acceptance in principle of the scientific methodology by most churches, the pressures have become subtler, weighing the balance of judgment in some scholars' minds in the direction of more conservative results, that is, toward conclusions less disturbing to traditional views.[12] To compromise with such pressures is to sacrifice the integrity of Biblical scholarship. The duty of the scholar is to reach his conclusions on the basis of the evidence no matter how disturbing they are to the mind of the church.

But sciences too have their orthodoxies. It is not only in

religion and theology that viewpoints which have received wide acceptance take on an exaggerated authority. In physics Einstein had to fight his way with his theory of relativity that demanded a radical reformulation of existing views. In economics there are conservatives and radicals, both claiming scientific validity for their principles. So also in Biblical science, by the time it had established itself in the churches and universities of the English-speaking world (in the first decades of the twentieth century), it had behind it more than a century of methodological discussions in which step by step the process of research had been widened to provide an accurate description of the history, literature, and religion first of Israel and then of the church in the Biblical period, and confidence in the resulting methodology was so strong that it had taken on the character of a scientific orthodoxy. Scholars who counted themselves liberals, or even radicals theologically, were stubbornly conservative in the face of any challenge to their "science" or to its "assured results." Against this background we can understand how disagreeable it was to critical scholars that at the very moment when they had finally established the validity of their science in the mind of the church, a voice should be raised challenging the adequacy of its hermeneutic and demanding a rethinking of the whole process of interpreting Scripture.[13]

For a few years the challenge was ignored since it came not from any recognized Biblical scholar but from an obscure Swiss pastor. The complaint was familiar, that the literary and historical analysis made it more difficult to preach from the Scriptures. This seemed to be just one more attack by the church on the integrity of the scientific interpretation of Scripture. Barth's two versions of his commentary on Romans were dismissed as eisegesis, a violent projection of a modern Kierkegaardian theology into Paul's text. Not until Rudolf Bultmann, who was recognized as one of the most accomplished and most radical New Testament scholars, joined his voice with Barth's and demanded a reopening of the discussion of hermeneutical principles did scholars begin to recognize how seriously their orthodoxy of method was being set in question.[14] In the English-speaking world the very hearing of the essential challenge was delayed, and in some quarters is still delayed, by the fact that Barth and Bultmann in the twenties and thirties became known primarily as the proponents of a so-called "dialectical theology" and the challenge to reopen the hermeneutical discussion became confused with the challenge of a new theological viewpoint. Distaste for the dialectical theology was illogically assumed to validate an ignoring of the new hermeneutical discussion. It is important therefore to recognize that the hermeneutical problem exists in independence of the large theological projects of Barth and Bultmann. It exists for anyone who attempts to interpret Scripture, no matter what his particular theological allegiance may be. These two scholars merely laid open new aspects of the problem of interpretation that had remained concealed from their predecessors. We have already noted that by 1920 Old Testament scholars were beginning to be disturbed that their methodology was resulting in a divorce of the Old Testament both from the New Testament and from the life of the church. In 1919, Rudolf Kittel, who was in no way the proponent of any new theology, called to the attention of his colleagues the strange and disturbing phenomenon, that their science seemed to be destroying the basis both for its own existence within a faculty of *Christian* theology and for the continued interest of Christian people in its findings.[15]

Both Barth and Bultmann were set thinking by their awareness of a decisive lack in the church's preaching. Barth in his Swiss parish found that his intensive training in exegesis under some of the most advanced Biblical scholars in Europe had not equipped him for his responsibility as "minister of the Word" to lay open the Scriptures week by week to his people as a word from God himself for their human situation. In fact, the whole manner of thinking that he had absorbed from his culture and from his most respected theological teachers seemed somehow to get in the way of his hearing what the Biblical witnesses had to say to him instead of sharpening his ears for hearing. A 180-degree adjustment in standpoint was needed for him to hear at all. Where he was accustomed to begin with man and work his way up to God, the Scriptures began with God and worked their way down to man. Something was seriously wrong with a hermeneutic that left him, and undoubtedly thousands of others like him, imprisoned and frustrated in such a dilemma. Bultmann had much the same undergraduate training as Barth but had gone on to become by 1920 one of the leading New Testament scholars in Europe. In 1921 he published his *History of the Synoptic Tradition,* in which he set down the results of his pioneering research in form criticism. But he suffered a similar distress to that of Barth. For him the heart of the New Testament was an absolutely unique life-transforming word from God to man. Through this word alone could man come to the fulfillment of his life as man. Without it all the values of his civilization were empty and his world was threatened with a return to chaos. The task of scholarship was to liberate this word on behalf of the church, but New Testament scholars, with all their magnificent accomplishments in language, literary analysis, historical reconstruction, comparative religion, and form criticism, were stopping short of this essential point and thereby failing the church in its most vital function, the preaching of its gospel.[16] Both Barth and Bultmann saw this hermeneutic failure not just as a problem of Biblical scholarship or of the church's preaching but as a crisis of humanity. The whole future of man was dependent upon the hearing of this word which was hidden in the New Testament.

Neither scholar had any intention of turning the clock back; neither had any complaint against the established principles of critical scholarship. Because Barth in his eagerness to get at the theological content of the text of Romans neglected many of the questions that had formerly received careful treatment in commentaries and because the focus of his interest was on Scripture as revelation, he was accused of disregarding the basic principles of exegesis. No one dared to make such an accusation against Bultmann. It puzzled Barth's critics that what seemed to them to be his conservative and reactionary tendencies did not inhibit him from going with Bultmann in even the most radical aspects of his form criticism. What they failed to grasp was that Barth and Bultmann were both of them on the pioneering edge of a new and necessary development in hermeneutics, not a reversion but an extension of the methodology of interpretation. Not a more conservative but rather a more radical and venturesome approach was needed to let the word of God hidden in the human words of Scripture have its freedom and power in the modern world. The failure of exegesis was not from what it did but from what it left undone. It was valid as far as it went, but it did not go far enough. It explored the linguistic, literary, historical, and religious dimensions of Scripture but left untouched the dimension where it becomes the medium of God's word and action in the life of man now. Thus far Barth and Bultmann were in agreement, but they differed in their understanding of what was needed to compass that ultimate dimension of Scripture.

Barth approached the problem as a theologian. To him the failure of the established hermeneutic to reach far enough was a theological failure. It was equipped to deal expertly with the problems of human language, human literature, human history, and all aspects of man's religious experience and practice but not with problems that arise when man stands in the presence of the living God. For several generations the Biblical scholar had been insisting that he was not a theologian but only a historian. It had seemed to him that he could be objective in his investigations only by divest-

Barth's response

ing himself of all theological preconceptions and interests. But what he actually accomplished was a limitation of his range of vision to the human phenomena of Scripture with only the most superficial probing of the theological depths of the text. Not that the Biblical "historians" succeeded in being untheological; their descriptions of the religion of Jeremiah, or of Paul, or of Jesus were full of theological overtones and undertones even when they managed to avoid the familiar theological terms. They were inadvertently rather than responsibly theological. Therefore what was needed was that the Biblical scholar should recognize the double character of his task: that because the Biblical text has both a historical and a theological content, he must be both a historian and a theologian, and as thoroughly equipped and critical in the one as in the other. Barth's criticism of the exegesis of his predecessors was that it was entirely too uncritical both in its own theological assumptions and in its descriptions of the theological content of Scripture. He found the source of much of the contemporary deafness to the voice of a Paul or a Jeremiah in the domination of men's minds (including his own) by theologies that were so completely at odds with the mentality of prophets and apostles that the distinctive witness of Scripture could no longer be heard or was so changed in the hearing that it lost its original meaning and power. His remedy was to listen, using every help that scholarship could provide, and to go on listening until the word within the words began to shape the ears and the mind congenial to it, with far-reaching consequences for theology and for man's life.

For Harrisville and the publican parable

Bultmann approached the problem primarily as a New Testament scholar. It seemed to him that what chiefly prevented the hidden word of the gospel from getting through into the church's preaching was the inappropriateness and incomprehensibility of New Testament language and thought forms in the modern world. The preacher, if he were a liberal, abandoned the mythological terminology and with it

Bultmann's response

abandoned the essential gospel, reducing it to a form little different from modern humanism or humanitarianism. But if he were a conservative, he kept all the New Testament terminology and by it conveyed meanings that had nothing in common with the original intention of the language. Therefore the remedy must be a new development in New Testament scholarship, an extension of the established hermeneutic, to go behind the mythological concepts of the New Testament to their intrinsic content and then to re-express that content in a language that would be readily comprehensible in a scientific and secular-minded age.

Because these two men diagnosed the problem differently and differed in the solutions they proposed, the developments that stemmed from each of them have from the beginning had a distinctive character and the influence of each has been quite different. While Barth has had a profound influence on some New Testament scholars—one has only to think of such persons in the English-speaking world as Sir Edwyn C. Hoskyns, C. K. Barrett, Paul S. Minear—his most conspicuous influence has been in the area of Old Testament theology. Bultmann, with his use of existentialist philosophy in order to solve the problem of translating mythological terms into modern language, has cut a narrower channel, restricted to the New Testament by his negative attitude to the Old Testament, and limited in range by the commitment to existentialism. This divergence has been the source of considerable confusion in the discussion of hermeneutics. Among the adherents of the "New Hermeneutic" whose interest is exclusively in the developments that stem from Bultmann, the tendency has been to give Barth credit for initiating the new discussion and then to proceed as though Bultmann and his disciples had been responsible for everything that has been achieved since that beginning.[17] The result is an unwarranted and unfortunate narrowing of the scope of the discussion and a concealment of some aspects of the problem.

three points of agreement

There are at least three points, however, at which Barth and Bultmann were agreed and which are basic to any new approach to the problem of interpretation.[18] First was their abandonment of the spectator attitude of their predecessors and a new approach to the subjectivity of the interpreter. For more than a century one of the chief aims of Biblical scholars had been to reduce the subjective factor in their investigations to an absolute minimum in order to secure the highest possible measure of scientific objectivity. The personal convictions, theological or philosophical, of the scholar were regarded as wholly disturbing elements, likely to interfere with the impartiality of the investigation. They were therefore to be set to one side while the scholar did his work. The whole history of interpretation, precritical but also critical, demonstrated how difficult it was for even the ablest minds to achieve impartiality. In the precritical centuries the distorting influence was mainly church tradition. But the critical scholar who freed himself of orthodox church tradition could find himself captive to some other cultural or philosophic tradition. Therefore the endeavor throughout the nineteenth century had been to perfect a methodology that on the model of natural science would enable the scholar to reconstruct the history and describe in detail the life and thought of each Biblical age as it actually occurred, undistorted by any preconception of his own. By the end of the century there was a generally held confidence that this capability had been achieved. Adolf von Harnack, as late as 1922, was shocked that anyone should question the ability of the historian to describe accurately the full content of Biblical religion. He himself in 1900 had offered a definition of the essence of Christianity that had received wide approval. To question the possibility of such objectivity seemed to him anarchic, an undermining of the foundations of all scholarly research and a surrender to the influence of human prejudice. But neither Barth nor Bultmann could any longer share this unlimited confidence.

cast aside attempt at objectivity

Harnack

Already among secular historians it was beginning to be recognized that every writing of history is an interpretation. The focus of interest, the choice of materials, the whole representation of the past, is always in some measure determined by the standpoint from which the author looks out upon the world. Man cannot look at man with the same kind of impartiality with which a geologist looks at a stone. Sooner or later it was bound to be recognized that, while each scholar was firmly confident of his own essential objectivity, his colleagues had little difficulty in detecting the influence upon his research of the cultural or theological context in which he did his thinking.[19] Harnack might regard his definition of Christianity as the product of impartial research but it required no remarkable critical ingenuity to detect the essentially Ritschlian theology with which he approached the New Testament. It seemed, therefore, to be a matter of simple honesty to acknowledge the presence of an interpretative context in every investigation and to take account of it as one of the factors in the total hermeneutic situation. Moreover, it was wrong to regard this subjective factor as wholly a negative and disturbing element in historical investigation. The historian's own personal involvement in the subject and his insight into men's statements about it in the past were the product of his grappling seriously in the present with the same problems with which they had to deal. In short, what the interpreter brings with him to the text can be the source not just of misunderstandings but also of his profoundest understanding.

What was rejected, then, was a spectator hermeneutic in which the scholar was under the illusion that he had attained an almost complete objectivity and remained unaware of the extent to which he was influenced by his own historical context. Certainly an almost complete objectivity was attainable in the determination of external facts, but a different approach was needed as soon as one began to probe beneath the surface into the depths of human life.

A spectator hermeneutic dissected the contents of ancient documents as the anatomist dissects a corpse, turning up a vast amount of valuable factual material but inhibiting any living converse with the authors of the documents. The interpreter had to withhold himself from all personal involvement with the author. But this means looking only from the outside at men who can be understood only from the inside, and keeping them at a safe distance instead of letting oneself and one's whole existence be set in question in confrontation with the ancient author. In a spectator hermeneutic the interpreter is master of the situation and, from his lofty throne above the flow of history, he is tempted to absolutize his own standpoint, to regard it as the culmination of all that has gone before and so to sit in judgment upon his author, assigning him his place on the ladder of progress at the top of which sits the enlightened scholar.[20] But the interpreter equally with the author has a historical context from which he cannot escape. He belongs not above but in the flow of history and is unwise to claim finality for any of his observations or judgments. The recognition of this involves no slackening in his commitment to impartiality, no license to let his preferences dictate his conclusions, but only an opening of the eyes to all the factors that belong in the relation between the author and the interpreter, that the author may escape the masterful grip of the spectator scholar and find his freedom to speak his mind to the modern age.

 A second point at which Barth and Bultmann were agreed was that interpretation has not completed its task until it has translated the content of the Scriptures out of their original language and thought forms into a language that is comprehensible to modern man. The established hermeneutic limited the task of the Biblical scholar to defining the original meaning of each text and giving a comprehensive description of Biblical religion in its successive stages of development. It was assumed that if Biblical science provided the reader with an accurate account of what the words meant when they were first used, he could without much difficulty translate the original meaning into a contemporary meaning. But this took no account either of the influence of the interpretative context on the investigation of the original meaning or of the distance between the text and the mind of modern man when all facile modernization is cut away and the text is allowed to recover its strange first accents. The question at issue here is whether the scholar is to consider his task finished when he has translated the words of the text accurately into the corresponding English words or whether he has responsibility to participate in the next stage of interpretation in which the theological content of the text is translated from the thought forms of the ancient world into those of our own time. I say *participate* because that profounder translation involves the systematic theologian, the homiletician, and the Christian educator. But it collapses if the Biblical scholar withdraws into the security of his descriptive science and refuses to go all the way with the preacher and the teacher on their journey from text to sermon or lesson. The reverse is equally true, that the translation will be ineffective unless the preacher and teacher are willing to spend time with the Biblical scholar in spelling out accurately the original meaning of the text.

A third point of agreement was that the ultimate and decisive content of Scripture is a revelation of God in which God comes to man in judgment and in mercy, setting him free from his past and opening to him a new future, and that this revelation is hidden in the text, inaccessible to the most attentive historian. Revelation is event, a divine event in the midst of history, unique so that access to it through the witness of the Scriptures is essential for every man if he is to find the fulfillment of the promise of his humanity. That it is event means that it is the presence of the living God with man and not a body of revealed knowledge transmitted from a distant God. Here Barth and Bultmann diverged. For Bultmann the hiddenness of God in his revelation meant that man knew God only in the change that was effected in his understanding of himself and his world. For Barth, while God is always hidden from man's mind, the event of revelation both in Scripture and in its present occurrence brings man not only to a new understanding of himself and his world but also to a knowledge of God, a knowledge of the God who is hidden but hidden to be revealed, and hidden still in every revelation of himself so that all knowledge of him is broken and incomplete. This divergence led Bultmann to the development of an anthropology rather than a theology and Barth to the development of what he liked latterly to call his theanthropology, an explication of man's broken knowledge of God which is at every step a knowledge of God with man and man with God. But what interests us here is the profound significance for hermeneutics and for the whole use of the Bible in the church of their joint insistence that, whatever else is heard from Scripture, the Scriptures have not yet spoken their essential word to man until in man's hearing of them God himself is found dealing with the human problem.

All three of these points are basic to the reopening of the hermeneutic question and we shall be concerned with them again and again in our discussion. Many of the impasses that the church faces in its use of Scripture are the consequence of a failure to take account of these elements in the relation between author and interpreter that were already laid open so competently a half century ago. Preachers and teachers have remained to a great extent at the level of a spectator hermeneutic and, imprisoned in it, have watched the Scriptures fade from public sight and interest.

IV

The Interpretative Context—*a natural appendage to the abandonment of the spectator attitude.*

THE INTERPLAY of subjective and objective factors in all our knowing has been so central a theme of philosophy through the centuries that it is surprising how consistently it has been ignored in the church's consideration of how Scripture is to be interpreted. It is not necessary here to trace the various theories: some reducing the human self to a blank sheet on which the world builds up its impressions, some reducing the world to an unknowable "thing" on which the mind of man projects its creations. For our purposes it is sufficient to recognize that the truth lies somewhere in between and that knowledge arises in the interaction of an inner world with an outer world. But because we look outward with our eyes rather than inward at what lies behind them we are more conscious of what the outer world contributes to our knowing than of the part that is played by elements behind our eyes.

All our knowing takes place in an interpretative context. This should be obvious to any preacher or to anyone who engages in public speaking. What the individual members of a congregation or audience are conscious of hearing is not to be equated with what was spoken. Each hearer receives the words of the speaker in a context of word meanings, general concepts, and his own accumulated experience and, since these differ with different persons who may come from widely varying religious and cultural traditions, the words spoken do not convey the same meaning to all who hear them. The preacher has constantly to consider not just what his own words say to him but also what they are going to say to his people. Only where speaker and hearers share a common tradition and have much in common in their interpretative contexts does the gap begin to be narrowed. Let their contexts be wide apart (a critical scholar in a conservative congregation or a Marxist philosopher in the United States Chamber of Commerce) and communication may break down entirely. But if the two listen patiently to each other over a period of time, they begin to discover much that they have in common in spite of all that divides them; they learn each other's differing use of the same words; they catch glimpses of each other's history and understand better why they differ; a common context is built up and communication becomes possible and even fruitful. Short pastorates have the disadvantage sometimes that, for lack of this common context, communication between preacher and people is barely begun. The graduate from seminary who does not recognize that the context he carries with him from seminary differs widely in language and interests from that of the members of the church of which he is now pastor is likely to be frustrated by a hidden wall that seems to shut him out from them, and at the same time he frustrates them with what seem to them his meaningless phrases.

We hear always in a context. The very mood of the listener may give the words an unintended meaning. An angry man hears accents that are provocative in a conversation with his friend and he may even claim to have heard words that were not spoken. We also see in a context of which we are not conscious. As we look down a long road, what actually meets our eyes is a road that grows ever narrower as it recedes into the distance. But we do not believe our eyes. We know from experience of the road that the two sides remain parallel and that it is distance that produces this distortion of reality. We do not even have to think about interpreting the images that meet our eyes. Unconsciously and instantaneously what we see is interpreted in the context of what we know to give us the road as it actually is. In our reading of books we are constantly made aware of the importance of the context in which we read. We have had the experience of finding a book, which we were quite unable to read a few years earlier, not only readable but intensely interesting in every sentence. It is not that in the interim we have become more intelligent but that our language, thought forms, and experience have been enlarged to enable us to share the thought world of the author. Without such sharing, his words are for us not media of communication but formidable barriers shutting us out from him.

It is obvious then that every man, scholar and layman alike, reads Scripture in an interpretative context. The meaning that seems to us to come directly from the words upon the page is actually an interpretation, the result of an instantaneous and unconscious process by which the words on the page receive specific meanings in our minds. The history of interpretation tells us what widely divergent meanings have been found in the same text by earnest men as they approached it, each with his own distinctive historical context. The interpretation does not begin when we sit down with the text and a number of commentaries to weigh the validity of a variety of suggested meanings. It begins before we are conscious of doing anything other than read the words. We hear them in a context, a highly complex context, the total context of our present historical existence. We hear them as the persons that we are, and their meaning for us is determined not only by the words but by the character of the context in which we receive them. No man has direct access to the content of Scripture either by the perfection of his scholarship or the power of his inspiration. Every apprehension of the text and every statement of its meaning is an interpretation and, however adequately it expresses the content of the text, it dare not ever be equated with the text itself. There remains always a significant distance between the interpretation and the text, a distance that counsels humility in the interpreter and excludes the absolutizing of any interpretation as though it were the final truth. It is striking how consistently interpreters of Scripture, ancient and modern, conservative and liberal, have ignored this basic principle of hermeneutics and have identified their interpretations directly with the content of the text.

It may be helpful for me to use my own experience with the Bible in illustration of the principle. The first context in which I read the Bible was provided for me by the church of my childhood and youth. The atmosphere was one of mildly conservative pietism, not aggressively fundamentalistic but certainly with no benefit of historical or critical knowledge. The Bible even in my private reading of it always spoke with a conservative and pietistic voice. It was assumed that that was the Bible's only voice, which was a burden to me for reasons that I did not then understand, but did not prevent me from hearing in it a message that shook my life to the depths and gave me at least the hope of becoming something other than the unsatisfactory being that I was. Then came years at college and in graduate school where I received a thorough training in historical-critical scholarship and learned to read the Bible as a complex of ancient religious documents. Under the guidance of my professors I formed a new context in which to read, which ostensibly was purely scientific and without theological presuppositions of any kind but actually was a blend of critical principles with liberal theology. The change of context generated problems of faith but was felt chiefly as a liberation from the cloying piety of the past. The Bible seemed a completely different book and spoke with a human freshness that it did not have before. The men and women of the Bible ceased to inhabit a never-never land somewhere between heaven and earth and came alive as creatures of flesh

this " moving from text to sermon" is the main theme of the book so far

and blood like myself, actors in a stream of human history that flowed from their door to mine. But the better I knew them the more they retreated into their ancient world with its strange customs and beliefs and the more difficult it became to extract from their religion values, ideals, and practices that were relevant in the modern world.

Then, after nine years of such training, I was plunged into a village pastorate where it was my task to interpret the Scriptures week by week to my people. I approached the task with confidence, for I had been grounded in the principles of exegesis. Knowing the original meaning of the text I expected it to be a simple matter to move from text to sermon. But it was not a simple matter. Something was wrong with the anchoring of the Bible in a liberal-historical context. There was a theological level in it beneath the literary, historical, and merely religious levels that my professors had somehow ignored (perhaps because the theology was discordant with their own), but in which I began to find a wealth of meaning for my people (none of the modern books on Old or New Testament theology had as yet appeared). As I listened, a new interpretative context took shape and the Bible became a very different book from what I had known before. Twice, then, within ten years I had to be liberated from contexts that were inadequate, yet each of the inadequate contexts had opened my ears to some portion of the reality of Scripture. The conservative-pietist context let me hear a penetrating word from beyond that challenged me to decision. The liberal-historical context made the Bible a very human book and taught me to listen for its original accents. These elements were carried forward into a new context that was shaped both critically and theologically simply by listening: listening as one committed to stand ever between the Scriptures as witness to the Word of God and a community famished for the bread of that word. But there was a warning in the experience not to absolutize any context. The conservative pietist considered his interpretation the only valid one and looked on the historical critic with suspicion and distrust. The historical critic was equally sure of the sole validity of his interpretation and was hostile to any suggestion that it might be superseded. But the Scriptures have a way of breaking through the contexts in which men seek to confine them, growing new ears in those who listen. And the process continues as the years advance. Life keeps creating new contexts and the dialogue with Scripture finds ever-new levels of understanding.

We have observed that the interpretative context, once established, recedes into the unconscious so that we cease to take account of it as a factor in our knowing. Insofar as it is taken over ready-made, or better, absorbed, from the environment and tradition in which life has placed us, we may be unaware that it is a relative historical product and consider it simply the normal way of healthy human seeing and hearing. We become dogmatic that what we see and hear is what everyone should be seeing and hearing. This has happened with a disconcerting regularity to interpreters of Scripture. Each interpreter has tended to identify what he has found in Scripture directly with the content of Scripture itself and to attribute to the interpretation the same authority that he assigns to the Scriptures. The interpretation then becomes a veil drawn over the surface of the text preventing the text from saying anything that would contradict the interpretation. It is easy for us to see this happening in the past. The rabbis of the time of Jesus had a traditional interpretation that enabled them to find in the Scriptures the authoritative validation of the beliefs, practices, and general structure of their religious community. The Scriptures being regarded as divine in every part and infallible, the same infallibility accrued to the interpretations that were identified with the Scriptures and the religious structures that were erected upon them. To contradict them in any way was blasphemy, for it was a contradiction of God himself. The consequence was that a community

how, then, can one respond to the question (after you have preached a brilliant and insightful sermon): that's good, reverend, but I disagree

imprisoned in such authoritative interpretations had no ears with which to hear a John the Baptist or a Jesus when in them the voice that had sounded in an Amos and a Jeremiah began to speak afresh. Moreover, those who most honored the Scriptures and studied them with the greatest diligence were the most severely afflicted with this deafness. The undevout outsider heard more readily.

The same thing happened in the sixteenth century. The earliest lectures of Luther show him using the traditional medieval hermeneutic, submissive to the modes of interpretation that had enabled the church of the preceding centuries to live comfortably with what it considered to be an infallible Scripture. Then in 1513, as he prepared his lectures on Romans for his students, he began to hear a different Paul from the one his predecessors had heard, a Paul who had been silenced by the traditional interpretations. In obedience to what he heard he had to change his whole method of interpretation. The Scriptures demanded a new interpretative context and a new hermeneutic. But it soon became evident that just as the medieval hermeneutic was part and parcel of the medieval structure of the church, the new hermeneutic let loose a gospel that called imperatively for a new kind of church and a new order of life. It is ironic that within a century of Luther's death his followers were attributing an authority to Luther's interpretation of Scripture which made it well-nigh unchallengeable and were insisting that God should always speak with the accents of Luther. The same thing happened with Calvinists. Calvin had left behind him a more comprehensive series of commentaries than Luther, remarkable still in their theological penetration, but the Calvinists of the next century under the authority of Calvin's name fastened on the Scriptures interpretations that no longer had the freshness of insight of the reformer. The Dutch theologian Cocceius complained that Calvinists would not be pleased to hear anything from Scripture that contradicted their interpretations.

Luther example

with your interpretation. (see p. 47)

Glaring examples of this transfer of authority from the Scriptures to the interpretation are to be found in the American religious scene where in some quarters the infallibility of Scripture has been made the central doctrine of Christianity, undoubtedly on the basis that all other doctrines derive their authority from their presence in an infallible Scripture.[21] A wide range of theological standpoints are to be found represented within this general orientation and each, because of its identification of itself with Scripture, claims for itself an infallibility! The resulting tensions can be severe. It is not unusual to find this insistence on inerrancy combined with a passionate rejection of any involvement of the church with political, social, or economic issues, or even used as a validation of the most brutal policies of racial discrimination. If we regard all this as conscious hypocrisy, we do not touch the edge of the problem. These are in many instances deeply earnest people who read their Bibles in a context which, to our mind, produces a grossly distorted gospel. There is no mystery about the forces that have shaped their interpretative context for them. They are the products of an aggressive capitalist economy with its individualistic philosophy of life, or of a society that has permitted the lines of racial distinction to harden into walls. Their way of reading Scripture has been subtly adapted to prevent any collision between what they hear in Scripture and the order of society that they prefer. They simply do not hear the consistent witness of the prophets to God's interest in the price the poor have to pay for grain and in the quality of justice in the law courts, in the foreign policy of the government, and in all man's acts of inhumanity toward his fellowman. They do not notice that Jesus stood directly in the tradition of the prophets and brought it to fulfillment in his own mission. They have what they call a spiritual Bible, which is concerned only with spiritual things such as God, the soul, and eternal life. Their interpretative context has silenced the unique and essential voice of Scripture in which the whole of God is concerned with the whole of man in the whole of life.

We see, then, that all interpretation takes place in a context and that no interpreter can escape from his historical context any more than he can jump out of his skin. The context furnishes at one and the same time the possibility of understanding and the possibility of misunderstanding. Its presence is more frequently unconscious than conscious and the interpreter is most under its influence when he is most unconscious of it. He can be totally unaware of it so that he identifies what the Bible means to him in his particular historical and theological context with what the Bible means absolutely. When this happens, he has robbed the Bible of its freedom to say anything that will be out of harmony with the milieu of his interpretation. The interpretative context with the hermeneutic intrinsic to it has seized the authority and has set boundaries to what the Scriptures are permitted to say. While ostensibly exalting the Scriptures, it has actually reduced the rich harmony of voices that make up the choir of Scripture to a single rather monotonous voice. As a result, the message of the Scriptures is dangerously narrowed, and many of its essential features are thereby silenced.

It is easy for us to recognize an illustration of this in an evangelist who prefaces his statements with the formula "The Bible says," but whose Bible never escapes from the limitations of the one particular stream of modern American Protestant religious tradition which he represents. But it may come as a surprise to find equally valid illustrations among venerable critical scholars. One of the functions of historical criticism has been to cut through the mass of traditional interpretations which have become fastened on the text of Scripture and expose to view the author's own intention. Basic to critical scholarship has been respect for the text and the willingness to let it speak its own mind no matter how many cherished theological conceptions or ecclesiastical structures it may endanger. But, in its determination to achieve a scientific objectivity comparable to that of the geologist, it came close at times to asserting almost complete independence of any interpretative context. The proud claim was voiced that it would make no difference whether the scholar were Christian, Jew, Mohammedan, agnostic, or atheist: if his critical principles were sound, he could achieve an accurate description of the Bible's content.[22] Invariably the statement of principle was left in the abstract, without the support of concrete examples of Christian, Jewish, Mohammedan, agnostic, or atheist exegesis! Concrete examples from existing literature would have set the principle seriously in question. There is indeed a factual level of considerable dimensions in Scripture on which such objectivity is possible. It can be maintained as long as the scholar remains a spectator of the Biblical scene and the Biblical text. But as soon as he moves from the outside to the inside and begins to probe the depths behind the text, it quickly becomes evident how impossible it is for him to contemplate man's life in another age from another vantage point than the one that happens to belong to him as the historical individual that he is. To claim for himself the same objectivity in his description of the prophetic or the apostolic faith as in his descriptions of the external world is to commit the same error as the evangelist, that is, to identify his evaluation of the content of Scripture directly with the actual content and to attribute to it a finality that it does not possess. Confidence in the scientific methodology provides the interpretation with an authority at times almost as confident as that which the evangelist derives from his belief in infallibility. Here again an authoritative interpretation is laid over the Scriptures and sets rigid boundaries to what may be heard from them.

To know how rigid these boundaries could become for scholars who prided themselves upon being open-minded scientists, perhaps one needs to have lived in the thirties of this century and to have rebelled against the established hermeneutic of his teachers. The dimensions of the "assured results" were awesome (many of them since then set radically in question) and to question either them or the methodology that had produced them was hazardous. Scholars differed sharply from each other on details of interpretation but always within the context of a generally accepted structure beyond which it was not wise to stray. Theology and its debates lay in that realm beyond. To let oneself become deeply involved in theological questions was regarded as likely to interfere with one's scientific objectivity. Religion as an observable phenomenon rather than theology was the focus of the Biblical scholar's interest. His task was to provide an accurate description of Israelite, Jewish, and early Christian religion, each in its proper setting in its ancient environment. If he chose to call the religious ideas theology, that was permissible, but there could be no theology of the Old Testament or of the New Testament or of the Bible as a whole since research had disclosed a variety of religious ideas or theologies in each of the Testaments. "Revelation" was an embarrassing word. It denoted the curious ancient idea that man could receive messages from the beyond. It made more sense when it was understood as a mythological way of expressing man's insights into meaning and truth. So also was the canon of Scripture an embarrassment, for it seemed unreasonable to draw a line around this particular selection of religious phenomena and religious literature as though all truth resided in them and none in the religions of man that happen to fall outside the line (or in the extracanonical literature of Israel itself).

Such judgments as these were assumed to be the findings of science and there was rarely any consciousness of the theological and philosophical assumptions that underlay them. Therefore when they began to be questioned in the twenties and thirties the resistance of Biblical scholars had in it at first the same kind of ferocity with which the funda-

mentalist defends his infallible Bible. But here and there
were scholars, no less scientific in their method, who recognized that something was seriously wrong with a hermeneutic that, in reducing the contents of the Bible to a curious
complex of ancient religious phenomena, was destroying in
Christians the expectation of hearing from it a decisive
word from God to man. *

Since the thirties the orthodoxies of the earlier period in
critical scholarship have been shattered. No one is any longer
inhibited in his theological interest. Gerhard von Rad, with
his exposition of the theological wealth and relevance of
Genesis, has no less respect for the text and no less competence in language, literature, and history than earlier com-
mentators. The theologies of the Old and New Testaments
that have appeared in such profusion in recent years do
not represent a decline in the quality of Biblical science
when compared with the presentations of Biblical religion
that preceded them, but rather an expansion of scope. The
publication of a massive *Theological Dictionary of the New
Testament* is not to be considered a disastrous development
merely because James Barr has been able to convict some of
its authors of semantic errors.[23] Old and New Testament
scholars have been wrestling with the problems inherent in
the movement toward a more adequate hermeneutic. Systematic theologians and philosophers have lent their aid.[24]
But there has been no single line of orderly development,[25]
perhaps in part because of the divergence between Barth and
Bultmann, perhaps in part because of a long-standing isolation of Old and New Testament scholars from each other,
but most of all as a consequence of a general neglect of the
hermeneutic issue. Scholars have been so intensely engaged
upon their own specific problems and programs that they
have failed to submit the underlying assumptions of their
own interpretative context to a sufficiently critical scrutiny.
It is here that they need the assistance of their colleagues
from systematic theology to bring clearly into the open the

*Some might argue: there is no decisive
word from God to man in the bible. It is
too diverse for there to be any decisiveness.

theological implications of those hidden assumptions.

The most notable feature of the North American scene has been the stubborn persistence of what we have called a spectator hermeneutic and the slightness of the attention that has been given to the problems that have become central among European scholars. In the forties and fifties there was a flurry of interest and "Biblical theology" attained a measure of popularity in some quarters, but it remained to too great a degree an imported product, echoing the European discussion rather than generating a discussion of basic issues between American Biblical scholars in which some common understanding might be reached concerning the character of Biblical scholarship as a theological discipline of the Christian church. For most American Biblical scholars the farthest they have moved is in describing the ultimate content of Scripture as theological rather than as merely religious. They would agree with Krister Stendahl that their discipline is a descriptive science that has completed its task when it has defined what the text of Scripture *meant* but has no responsibility in relation to what the text *means*.[26] To introduce the question of present meaning seems to them not only to complicate the task needlessly but to destroy the possibility of objective scientific research. The task of translating the content of Scripture into contemporary language and thought forms Stendahl assigns wholly to the systematic theologian and the preacher. The Biblical scholar determines scientifically the original meaning of Scripture and then entrusts to others the difficult journey from the ancient to the modern world. Whether or not they reach the modern world without losing the precious meaning is not his responsibility. He need not consider it a function of his discipline that he should accompany them on their journey.

V

The Permission
of Ignorance

PROTESTANT CHURCHES have traditionally made much of the fact that they have put the Bible into the hands of the common people and have pointed the finger of scorn at a Catholic church that in fear of the consequences withheld the Bible from its people. That basis for an attitude of superiority is now vanishing. But it would have vanished long ago if Protestant churchmen had opened their eyes to the fact that in actual practice they were withholding from their people the tools a modern man needs in order to understand the Bible—for fear of the consequences! Historical criticism has been with us now for over two hundred years. It arose as the forces of the Enlightenment in the eighteenth century put an end to the blind acceptance of merely traditional knowledge in every area of life and freed men's minds to investigate the universe afresh. It was only a matter of time until the discovery of Copernicus and Galileo that the earth goes round the sun would displace the old earth-centered universe. And it was no honor to Catholics or Protestants that they united in resisting the new knowledge. But, equally, it was only a matter of time until the centuries-old view that Moses wrote the Pentateuch would have to surrender to what men's eyes told them when they let the text of the Pentateuch tell its own story—that it is a complex of ancient traditions that came into its final form nearly a millennium after the time of Moses. Historical criti-

religious people who fear truth.

cism consists simply in the endeavor to let the whole Bible from beginning to end tell its own story with the assistance of all the other knowledge that modern investigation has brought to light. But because that story frequently contradicts the old traditional views and presents a different picture from what one reads off the surface of the Scriptures, it has from the beginning been regarded with nervousness by churchmen, if not with outright hostility. The whole bench of Anglican bishops in England in 1861 condemned the authors of *Essays and Reviews* for dabbling in historical criticism and the General Assembly of the Free Church of Scotland in 1881 dismissed its ablest historical-critical scholar, W. Robertson Smith, from his chair in Aberdeen for the same offense. We are ashamed of those events, futile defenses of ignorance against an irresistible advancing tide of knowledge, but the shame would be more fruitful if it took account of the degree to which a continuing nervousness about the results of historical criticism has permitted a gross ignorance about the Bible to persist in the membership of the church right down to the present day.

We smile when we hear of a Flat Earth Society, an organization of people who ostensibly in faithfulness to the Scriptures have banded themselves together to preserve the Biblical view that the earth is flat, and we laugh at the havoc created for them by the recent pictures of our globe from outer space. But most of our churches have engaged in a disturbingly similar maneuver in leaving their members to read the Bible with a naïveté that becomes increasingly vulnerable as the advances in modern education and mass communication bring the whole population abreast of modern knowledge. A Bible that is left in the medieval world and a membership that has moved on into the modern world are not likely to have much to say to each other. That tragic gap could have been prevented if the whole church had been allowed to move with its scholars out of the naïveté and literalism of the past into a frank and honest facing of the problems that the text of Scripture provides for the modern mind.

We can understand, then, why some analysts of the situation who profess great zeal for the Bible regard historical criticism not as a factor in keeping the Scriptures central in the life of the church and stimulating the interest of Christians in them, but as a primary influence in undermining their authority, creating disrespect for them, and contributing to their neglect in preaching. They are a carry-over from a time not too far behind us when "higher critics" was a term of abuse and the idea was widespread that they were a race of skeptics invading the church who were tearing the Bible apart and destroying all confidence in its revelation. But, in spite of abuse and the occasional expulsion of a scholar from his chair, they went quietly on with their investigation of the language, literature, history, religion, theology, and the whole complex background of Biblical life. Today these higher critics are no longer maligned except in the most backward churches that have let themselves be victims of a cultural paralysis. They occupy almost all the chairs of Old and New Testament in theological seminaries and faculties thoughout the world. They have produced a vast library of dictionaries, commentaries, monographs, and periodicals that explore in the minutest detail every aspect of the Scriptures. Most churches today know that the so-called higher critics are simply Christians who are devoting their time and talents to the study of the Scriptures and to the production of literature that will help people everywhere to read the Scriptures with understanding. As a result of their labors there now exists a vast fund of resources for the study and interpretation of the Bible in the church. And yet! And yet the membership of the church to a very large extent has been allowed so far as the Bible is concerned to remain far into the twentieth century at a level of knowledge which would be more appropriate to the seventeenth century.

The resources accumulated by scholarship have remained

"a twentieth-century church with a seventeenth-century mind."

largely bottled up in the classrooms and libraries of theological seminaries. Only in a tiny trickle have they made their way down into the life of local congregations. Most church members even in the most progressive churches are to this day unaware that they exist. There are three major channels that should have served the flow of knowledge—the pulpit, the church school, and a church library with an active program for the circulation of its books. To begin with the last, only a small number of churches are alert to what can be accomplished in lay education by introducing their people to books. Some that have libraries leave it to chance whether anyone ever makes use of them. But in most churches not one modern book that would be of practical value in overcoming Biblical ignorance is available to the members, or even to the church school teachers. Also it is notorious how rarely the official church magazines that go into the homes of the people review books of this character.

The second factor, the church school, has had a heavy responsibility either for perpetuating the old naïveté or for introducing the historical and critical viewpoint in a timid and cautious fashion that was unlikely to generate either interest or confidence. As recently as twenty-five years ago some of the major Protestant churches on this continent were still nervous about allowing critical problems to be discussed in the literature provided for the church school. Those responsible were well aware that from the standpoint of honest scholarship their policy was indefensible. They also knew that teachers were bombarded with literature from conservative sources that equated faithfullness to the Scriptures with the rejection *in toto* of the fruits of historical criticism. But the peace of the church was valued more highly than truth. The consequences of leaving a twentieth-century church with a seventeenth-century mind were ignored. The policy in many instances was deliberately followed of leaving teachers and pupils ignorant of the resources of knowledge that were already available with which to meet the

"... crying peace, peace, when there is no peace."

questions that the twentieth-century mind keeps asking concerning the Scriptures. One of the most disconcerting experiences of my lifetime was the discovery in 1948 of how many reputable church officials and men who were regarded as leaders could still at that late date counsel a timid concealment of knowledge in the interests of harmony when a new Presbyterian educational program proposed that Biblical study in the local congregation come fully abreast with Biblical study in the church's theological seminaries. It was regarded as a great victory when official permission was given that the church's educational literature should at last be completely honest with children, young people, and adults in its approach to the problems of Scripture!

The third channel through which such knowledge should have reached the church was the pulpit. For fifty years now men trained in most of our theological seminaries have been receiving a thorough grounding in the methods and values of historical criticism. For many of them it has opened the Bible to them with a freshness that has been liberating. Yet few of them have let their congregations share this knowledge with them in the course of their preaching and teaching. They have let the Bible of their people remain in a context that it no longer has for them themselves. Not that they needed to preach sermons on pentateuchal analysis or on the Synoptic problem, but only that in incidental ways they could have opened the eyes of their people to the problems that were there for them in Scripture and let them know that an intelligent approach to such problems clears the way for a more fruitful listening to the text. Many people do not even know that the church is awake to the existence of the problems that they themselves find so disturbing about the Bible. The church as they know it has more facility with answers and solutions than with the recognition of problems. In fact, sometimes the impression is conveyed that the church is not the place to ask questions, particularly about the Bible.

Quite recently one of our North American churches, which in most aspects is eagerly progressive but which had long delayed the recognition of critical problems in its approach to Scripture in Christian education, introduced a new church school curriculum that was committed to deal frankly with historical and literary questions. At last children were to be allowed to know that the two stories of Creation in Genesis are best understood as something other than history. Two or even perhaps three Isaiahs made their appearance. But as soon as the new literature was published, it was met by a storm of protest and generated a vigorous public discussion. In one village three men, prominent in the local church, were standing in the street reviewing the situation with some concern when a retired minister, who had been their pastor many years before, joined them. They told him what they were discussing and received from him the assurance that there was nothing really new or disturbing in the approach of the curriculum to the Bible. "We had it all in seminary fifty years ago," he said, to which the immediate retort of one of the men was, "Then why in hell didn't you tell us about it?" He had preached for years in the village church without anything of what he knew concerning a historical approach to Scripture getting through to the people who listened to him Sunday by Sunday! The permission of ignorance!

Why has there been this withholding of knowledge which has created a paralyzing gulf between the seminary and the pew? Fear has played a part. After the General Assembly of the Presbyterian Church in the U.S.A. in 1893 dismissed Charles Augustus Briggs from its ministry for denying that Moses wrote the whole of the Pentateuch, most pastors would be rather cautious in speaking of Moses. Why disturb the minds of people with questions of authorship? And why risk being driven from one's church on such an issue? Was there not an abundance of material in the Bible on which one could preach without ever having to touch upon any historical-critical problem? Fear can sometimes masquerade as prudence. But closely allied with fear was a false conception of what is necessary or desirable for a layman. It was easy to tell oneself that, although the most progressive Biblical and theological scholarship was essential for a minister, there was no need to distress and confuse the minds of laymen with questions that are debated more appropriately in seminary classrooms. What more did a layman need from the Scriptures than the simple elements of the gospel that would acquaint him with God's grace toward him and God's will for his daily life? But this was a gross miscalculation and has alienated from the church thousands of Christians who cannot endure a weekly reminder of this underestimate of their intelligence.

In fairness to such cautious pastors, however, we have to recognize that many of them were sent out ill-equipped to take a congregation all the way from a naïve, uncritical, unhistorical reading of the Scriptures to an understanding of them that, by an intelligent use of modern resources, would enrich and deepen their impact. As we have already seen, they may have been trained in a scholarship that was stronger in analysis than in synthesis, more focused on literary and historical criticism than on theological content, and unaware of the rough road that has to be traveled from the definition of what the text *meant* to the definition of what it *means*. The average scholar does not appreciate how devastating his critical analysis can be to the preacher. Wilhelm Vischer, in his *The Witness of the Old Testament to Christ*,[27] points out how the stories of the patriarchs in Genesis for thousands of years interested and instructed the generations of both Jews and Christians but in the hands of the literary critics fell silent. It was fascinating to disentangle the strands of tradition of which they were composed and to set each story in its ancient context, but the more thoroughly scholarship did its work the more distant the patriarchs seemed to be from any useful contact with modern man. Vischer's contention was that this is a scholarship that stops halfway. It has failed to go beneath the literary and historical levels of the text to the theological intention where Abraham, Isaac, and Jacob begin to take on relevance for the church of today.

The Book of The Acts furnishes an excellent illustration from the New Testament. The preacher sees here an opportunity to take his people back into the earliest Christian church, to listen to the preaching of Peter and Paul, and to witness the triumphs of the gospel in the era of its birth. He assumes the author to be Luke, who as the companion of Paul and as a visitor to Palestine was not far removed from the events that he was reporting. He can find commentaries that leave him undisturbed in this approach to The Acts, but a more thorough criticism dissolves it piece by piece. The attitude to Paul's status as an apostle, the account of his movements after his conversion, the representation of his relation with the Jerusalem church and of his preaching to Gentiles, are so different in The Acts from what they are in his letters that it seems impossible that the author of The Acts should have been a close associate of Paul. The speeches of The Acts, like the speeches in all Greek histories, are not verbatim reports of apostolic preaching but rather are representations of how an author near the end of the first century conceived the preaching of Peter and Paul. The Book of The Acts comes to us not directly from the Church of the apostles but from the following generation, the subapostolic church, when the divergent streams that appear so clearly in Paul's letters had been merged into one stream and old conflicts and divisions were forgotten. The preacher's task seems so much simpler if he can ignore these findings of critical investigation. They appear at first to rob him of The Book of The Acts as material for his preaching—but only when he stops too soon. The book still takes him back into the first-century church even when criticism has done its work in the reconstruction of the history, but into a far more complex and humanly believable church than appears on the surface of the text, a divided church that had to find its unity, a limited church that only gradually came to recognize the full scope of its mission and the far-reaching implications of its gospel. If, however, one examines the commentaries on The Acts that are available in the English-speaking world, one is struck by the way in which most of them evade the sharpness of the critical problems, assuming that Luke was the author and reading the sermons of Peter and Paul as though they were directly from the lips of the apostles. They seem much too anxious to placate the simple traditional view to be of any use to a church that has to hear the message of the text from *beyond* the full consequences of the most ruthless criticism if it is to hear it at all. A historical criticism that is afraid of being too destructive by being too thorough and therefore seeks some form of respectable compromise with entrenched traditional interpretations does nothing to help the church's membership make the transition that has already been accomplished in the realm of scholarship.

In order to understand why this transition has been particularly difficult to make in the American churches, we need to review briefly the history of Biblical interpretation in this century and to see what its distinctive character has been in America. It is a serious mistake to think that historical criticism has always and everywhere had the same character. It has gone through great changes in the course of its history and it exists in a variety of forms today. At the turn of the century in Germany it had already more than a hundred years of development behind it and had reached what to most scholars seemed to be its definitive form. It was a historical science, committed to the same principles of literary and historical investigation that were obligatory for all historians and free from all theological or ecclesiastical dictation in reaching its conclusions. Its task was to lay bare the whole complex of life, thought, and religion that comes to expression in the two Testaments. In order to achieve scientific objectivity it focused its attention upon the phenomena of Hebrew, Jewish, and Christian religion rather than on the relation between God and man that gave rise to these differing forms of religion.

In Britain at the turn of the century historical criticism had a character quite different from this. Where in Germany it was in general divorced from theology and from the life of the church, in Britain it was usually allied in its beginnings with an evangelical theology that was mildly and not radically liberal. Its representatives were men such as James Denney, B. F. Westcott, George Adam Smith, Bishop Gore, and many others who were churchmen before they were scholars. They were deeply concerned that the Scriptures, by being more intelligently understood, should come more adequately to expression in the preaching of the church. Their interest in historical and critical problems was subordinate to a theological concern. This may at times have made them less boldly critical than they might have been, but it anchored their scholarship securely in the life of the church and facilitated its acceptance by clergy and people.

In America at the turn of the century historical criticism was only beginning to make its way,[28] twenty-five years later than in Britain, and it took its character partly from German influence and partly from British, but the more powerful and sustained influence then and later was to be from Germany rather than from Britain. Various factors contributed to this. In an America increasingly fascinated by the promise of what was to be achieved by the application of strictly scientific method, the methodology of German scholarship had the stronger appeal. British scholarship with its mingling of critical and theological concern was similar to what the German had been at an earlier stage, before that stage was transcended in the interests of scientific method. Was it not also clear that the front line of pioneering research in both Testaments was in Germany rather than in Britain, so that it was naturally to Germany that graduate students would go for advanced training? Another important influence arose from the passionate and brutal assaults that American critical scholars had to endure from conservative churchmen. In Germany since early in the nineteenth century there was a form of historical criticism practiced by conservative scholars such as Beck and Von Hofmann and in Britain it had long been clear that one could be both critical and evangelical. But in America a false dichotomy was established between the terms "critical" and "evangelical." Evangelical Christianity very widely committed itself to a doctrine of literal inerrancy that forbade the use of historical criticism and branded those who used it as enemies of the Bible and therefore enemies of God. This either threw the critical scholar into firm alliance with theological liberalism, which seemed to be the only alternative to such conservatism, or made him take refuge in a department of Oriental literature where in his purely academic capacity he had no responsibility for theological matters. There was a protection from attack in being untheological.

It is rather ironic that in the twenties and thirties of this century historical criticism in America should have been consolidating its purely scientific and untheological stance at the very time when in Europe Biblical scholars were moving on toward a new recognition of their inescapable theological involvement and responsibility. The European development hardly touched the American scene until after the war of 1939-1945 and even then its influence was hindered by its association with the name of Barth, whose theology continued to be distasteful to most American theologians. Interest in the theological aspects of interpretation was confined to a small number of scholars, many of whom were interested also in Barth's theology. Then, as we have seen, in the sixties it began to be evident that the earlier spectator hermeneutic was still dominant, that the theological development was receding rather than advancing, and that the discussion of hermeneutics was being turned almost wholly into a Bultmannian channel. The continued strength of the earlier untheological viewpoint was evident in a recent meeting of the Society of Biblical Literature. The editor of the society's journal, in making his annual report, defined his policy in some such words as these: "All of you know the basis on which I edit the Journal. Its interest is confined to the philological, literary, and historical aspects of Biblical investigation. If papers are sent in that deal with theological or homiletical topics, I send them back unread in the next mail." From the hundreds of Old and New Testament scholars in attendance there was no word of protest. Certainly some were unhappy with the statement, but they felt themselves so completely in the minority that it seemed futile to ask even for a discussion of the policy.[29]

The forces making for this resistance to theological responsibility are multiple. An increasing number of Biblical scholars are in the rapidly expanding departments of religion in universities where they feel much more comfortable and secure as historical and literary scientists than as theologians. Then there is the whole background of American scientific achievement, the consciousness of leading the world in the application of science in every area of life, and, perhaps, a growing unwillingness to be led by the nose down whatever road European theologians and Biblical scholars may choose to take. W. F. Albright, famous for his achievements in archaeology and for his training of so many outstanding Old Testament scholars, considers himself strictly a historical scientist even in his forays beyond archaeology into Biblical interpretation and theology. His prospectus for The Anchor Bible series made much of the "purely scientific" character of the work.[30] Add to this the fact that few American systematic theologians have shown any interest in Biblical theology. Philosophical theology dominating the American situation, there has naturally been little encouragement from that quarter for Biblical scholars to spell out the implications of the Scriptures for theology today. With such forces as these at work and with the discussion of hermeneutics so halting and confused as it has been, it is not surprising that American Biblical scholarship has remained largely a "descriptive science" and as such stops short of the point where it can command the time and interest of the preacher and the ordinary Christian. It claims for itself a character that anchors it in the academic world and prevents it from being a necessary and indispensable day-by-day function of the church. Because of this it has unintentionally made a massive contribution to the continuing ignorance of the Bible in the membership of the church.

VI

The Theological Significance
of Historical Criticism

WE HAVE been attempting to diagnose a breakdown in
communication between the Bible and the church and
have found the source of the breakdown in a kind of ecclesiastical schizophrenia. With one lobe of its brain, the scholarly lobe, the church has moved out of the precritical era to an
acceptance, albeit at times a grudging acceptance, of historical criticism, but with the other lobe of its brain, which extends widely through its membership, it remains in the precritical era. The hiatus between the two has been sharpened
by the inability of historical criticism, at least in the form
that has been widely accepted, to take adequate account
of the theological content of Scripture. And now, when a
new development has taken place in interpretation which
would extend the scope of historical criticism in order to
let the theological content have its full significance, and
with the prospect in sight of overcoming the hiatus in the
mind of the church, Biblical scholarship in America, in
fear of losing its scientific character, resists any extensive
modification of its hermeneutic.

It is a mistake, however, to think that a spectator hermeneutic is more scientific than a responsibly theological one.
A scientific methodology for the investigation of any subject matter must be determined by the character of the subject matter. The inadequacy of historical criticism in its
earlier form became evident in its inability to deal with Scrip-

ture as witness to a unique and life-transforming revelation of God to man. In order to bring the subject matter under control it had to reduce it to a complex of literary and historical traditions exhibiting a series of developments in human religion. But that reduction removed from sight the one element in the Bible that has been responsible for its centrality and authority in the Christian church. The subject matter in Scripture is more than literature, history, and religion; it is a witness that extends over more than a thousand years to a relationship between God and man in which, first in Israel, then in Jesus Christ and his church, the deepest mysteries of man's life in time and beyond time were revealed. The Scriptures are a theological as well as a historical entity and they demand for their scientific investigation a methodology that is as responsible theologically as it is historically. We must guard, however, against thinking of the historical and theological elements in interpretation as though they existed in separate compartments, the theological being an additional compartment added on to an untheological historical one. The theological and the historical content of Scripture are not two separate realities but are one reality with two aspects, each inseparable from the other and interfused with it. The historical scholar who disclaims theological responsibility is simply closing his eyes to the theological aspects and implications of his research. Because the text upon which historical criticism is focused is theological in character, the investigation of it has had profound theological significance even when it has been most avowedly untheological.

A valid criticism of Karl Barth's approach to Scripture is that he makes too sharp a separation between historical and theological interpretation.[31] The former he assigns only a preparatory function, a kind of clearing of the deck for the essential interpretation which is theological. He has always made explicit his acceptance of the basic principles of historical criticism. His one objection was to its failure to transcend its preparatory function and so its neglect of the theological content which alone has caused the Biblical documents to survive the centuries. His own concern, therefore, was to get on with what to him was the primary task of exegesis, the exposition of the theological content. The preparatory stage was being sufficiently cared for by others. But the effect of this approach, and especially of the categorizing of historical and literary research as merely preparatory, was to create the impression that the historical and theological aspects of interpretation could exist in separation from each other. It was only a short step from this, for some who came under Barth's influence but had not his thorough training in historical critical scholarship, or who had grown up in an atmosphere hostile to such scholarship, to assume that now a happy era had arrived in which, unencumbered by the problems of historical and literary criticism or comparative religion, they could proceed directly to the excavation of the theological content of the text. They were further encouraged by Barth's use of analogy and typology in his interpretation to reintroduce not only analogy and typology but also allegory as legitimate devices in extracting an edifying meaning from the text,[32] so that theological interpretation seemed to be on the way backward toward the Middle Ages.

One can understand the effect of this in creating a reaction against theological interpretation and a renewed emphasis upon the importance of the historical task. But among Old and New Testament scholars who have been foremost in the recognition of their theological responsibility there has been no sign of any inclination to separate the theological from the historical or to depreciate the importance of literary and historical research. The relation between the two aspects of interpretation is one of the primary problems of hermeneutics at which we shall have to look more closely. It is still in need of exploration and illustrates the unfinished character of the new development. It needs always to be kept in mind that old and new forms of hermeneutics do not as yet stand over against each other, clearly defined. We see the earlier one with greater clarity because it has been at work in our midst for some time in a fully matured form. We can evaluate its successes and its failures, its positive and its negative contributions in the life of the church. But the later, more recent, developments are still in process and the hermeneutical discussion today is the attempt to find the way from a hermeneutic that has demonstrated certain crucial inadequacies to one that will let the Bible recover its living voice in the church and, through the church, in the world. Every angle of the problem has to be explored but always with the realization that ultimately a new methodology will be hammered out, tested, and perfected not primarily in discussions of hermeneutical principles but in the exegesis of the text of Scripture itself.[33]

One of the first demands of historical criticism is respect for the text of Scripture and a determination to get at not only the earliest form of the text but the original meaning of that earliest text. Textual criticism in its search for the earliest form of the text has since the time of Origen commanded the interest of scholars but has received fresh impetus from the discovery at Qumran of texts a thousand years more ancient than any that were formerly available. Already in textual criticism when a comparison is made between variant texts, as, for instance, between the Greek and the Hebrew texts of the Old Testament, a theological element becomes evident. Subtle shifts in meaning took place as the translators who lived in a Hellenistic world prepared the Biblical text for its appearance in a Hellenistic costume. So also, the translation of the Bible into Latin shows at certain points an accommodation of the text, which was not necessarily conscious, to the forms, the doctrines, and the practices of the church. The translations had a context. We see it more clearly in translations that were made at a distance from us such as the Greek and Latin and less clearly in translations whose context is closest to our own. Translation is always in some degree interpretation and is then followed by an exegesis in which the mind of the interpreter meets and seeks to understand the mind of the author.

In the past there has always in exegesis been a struggle between the theology of the Biblical author and the theology of the interpreter. In the Middle Ages the authors were worsted since the interpreters by the use of allegory were able to find in the text almost any meaning that they desired. Luther, Calvin, and other Reformers, while they cannot be called historical critics, can, however, be regarded as forerunners, along with Erasmus, because of their respect for the original Hebrew and Greek text and their zeal to uncover the meaning of the original text from under the heap of misinterpretations that the centuries had placed upon it. In many instances a new translation from the Hebrew or Greek was the equivalent of a new interpretation and was sufficient to let the text speak with revolutionary power. But none of the Reformers saw the danger of their own interpretation becoming a new form of imprisonment for the text or the need to establish a methodology in interpretation that would safeguard the freedom of the text. It was not until two centuries later when the Bible had become largely a reservoir of proof texts for the doctrinal systems that had been extracted from it and was no longer allowed to speak for itself, that a renewed respect for the text began to bring historical criticism into existence. Pietism and the evangelical revival had turned men back to the Bible to find in it what they could not find in the rigid doctrinal formulations of the various orthodoxies of the time but had given no attention to the problem of how to guard against misinterpretation. That was left to more coldly rational scholars who saw that only the most careful study of the Biblical language and the unearthing of the original meaning from beneath the traditional interpretations could provide the text with its freedom and the scholar with a crite-

[handwritten margin note: a history of the development]

rion for distinguishing between interpretation and misinterpretation.

The problem was much more complex than was realized at first, or, for that matter, for long afterward. It was expected that with the application of a scientific methodology it would be possible to establish the literal meaning of Scripture with a finality that would be incontestable. We have seen how that expectation was disappointed. Albert Schweitzer, in his *The Quest of the Historical Jesus*, has illustrated for us vividly the limitations that historical criticism experienced in its first century.[34] Nevertheless, principles were being established to safeguard the text against manipulation, principles that cannot be disregarded or neglected without opening the door to a flood of irresponsible interpretation. One of the most important consequences of this respect for the text and guarding of its freedom was the recognition that there must ever be a distance between the text and the interpretation that is placed upon it. Before the rise of historical criticism, Biblical theology and systematic theology were all of a piece. The church's theology, based on the Scriptures, was assumed to be the theology of the Scriptures. But now the distance between the two came into sight. The Biblical authors were freed to be men of their own time in their theology and the systematic theologian was freed to be a man of his own time in his theology.[35]

A second major contribution of historical criticism theologically to the church has been its demonstration of the humanity of the Scriptures. Just as the misunderstanding of the divinity of Jesus leads to an obscuring of his humanity, so the misunderstanding of the sacredness of the Scriptures obscures the full human character of the text and removes it into a world other than the one that we inhabit. Docetism gives us a Jesus who is no longer one of us and can no longer make us one with him for our redemption. And parallel with that, it gives us a Bible before which we stand in such awe that we fail to enter into intimate converse with those who speak to us by means of it. The text becomes a static formulation of divine truth rather than the human historical words of men like ourselves.

The tendency in the church toward docetism has always been strong because of the elements in Scripture that encourage it. There is an externalizing of the divine presence and action that takes place in the traditions in both Testaments, a describing of events that occurred in the personal relation between God and man as though they had been visible events. God walks the earth in visible form and holds conversations with men. He appears to Moses in a burning bush that the reader assumes anyone could have seen had he been present. The descent of the Spirit upon Jesus at baptism becomes in John's Gospel a visible movement in space which the prophet John observes. Miraculous interventions are constantly occurring. The difference between that world and ours is obvious. We live in a realm where Jesus was crucified and God did not intervene, where six million Jews were burned in gas ovens and there was no *Psalm 13* miracle to save them, where God is hidden from the eyes of men so completely that only faith can know his presence, and where nothing ever interrupts the order of nature. In short, we live in the flow of history and unless the men who meet us and speak to us in the Scriptures lived in the same flow of history, we have nothing in common with them and they have nothing in common with us. Docetism breaks the continuity between Biblical history and our history, removes that uniquely important segment of human history into a realm of its own, and thereby destroys the possibility of effective communication from there to here. Historical criticism, therefore, performs an invaluable service theologically when it strips away all mythological concealment from Israelite and early Christian history and, placing it firmly in its context in the larger history of the ancient Near Eastern world, establishes its continuity with our world and our history.[36]

third
contribution

Closely related to this is the relativizing of everything human and historical that puts an end to even the subtlest forms of idolatry. Idolatry results from a confusion of the temporal with the eternal, the human and earthly with the divine. In its crude forms it long ago ceased to be a problem of the church, only to reappear in a more deceptive form in the direct identification of the truth of God with some human phenomenon: the dogmas of the church, the words of a pope, or a sacred book. There is a powerful urge in men, even in Christian men, to give God visibility,

yes!

to have something in their human world and in their hands that is divine. It is not enough for them that absolute truth resides in God; they must have a portion of it in their own hands and at their disposal: God visible and available, God securely installed within the human institution to make its authority over men absolute and unchallengeable. There have been both Protestant and Catholic forms of this idolatry. But historical scholarship, when it is allowed its full exercise, exposes ruthlessly the relativity of everything historical, puts an end to the absolutizing of anything human, and restores the distance between God and man, between the temporal and the eternal. There are no absolutes in time. From the beginning to the end of time all is time-conditioned.

The Christian is reluctant to include Jesus in this "all." Is he not for us the one point of absolute truth in the whole of history? How we answer is important, for even here at this point we can fall into idolatry. The absolute truth of God in Jesus Christ is hidden in his history to be revealed to faith. In his humanity Jesus of Nazareth participates in the relativities of history. He was a Jew of the first century A.D., conditioned in his speech and conduct by the language and customs of his time and place. He observed the Jewish festivals, worshiped in the Jewish synagogue, and could argue at times like a rabbi. He can be understood adequately only when his words and actions are observed in their Jewish setting. But that in no way contradicts the Christian faith in him as uniquely one with God or the reality of the divine action in him for man's redemption.

The ruthlessness with which the historian exposes the relativity of everything human has been and still is a source of great distress to many churchmen. To them it seems as though the Christian faith were without any solid foundation unless somewhere in the sea of historical relativity they can put their hands with assurance on absolute truth. But different churches have located their formulation of absolute truth at different points in history and wherever they have located it they have anchored the church to the mentality and spirit of that time. The foundation of the church according to the New Testament was nothing visible or tangible but was the risen Lord, a spiritual presence in the midst of his people to provoke in them, as they remembered his earthly ministry, a renewal of his spirit and his mission. He left behind no formulations of doctrine, no structures of church life, no sacred writings, that a later age could absolutize, for he had himself grown up in a static religious order that had become an obstacle to the progress of God's redemptive purpose for man. And yet his church again and again in its history was to reproduce that static religious order, and, paralyzed by it, lose its freedom to move out in the service of God into an uncharted future. Therefore, the historian's relativizing of everything human, in Scripture and far beyond the Scriptures, far from being a threat to the church, can actually be a liberation of the church from outworn formulas of the past to let itself be led by the word and spirit of God into a new stage in the unfolding of its destiny.

An aspect of historical criticism which might not at first be reckoned as theological but which actually is the very soul of theology is its demand for honesty, intellectual integrity, in all our dealings with Scripture. We must let the facts be what they are.[37] Dishonesty takes subtle forms: a closing of the eyes at certain moments or to certain elements in the phenomena that are before us, a twisting of the facts to make them fit our theory or support our practice, a coloring of the facts to make them appear other than they are. It happens in personal relationships and destroys the integrity of the relationships. It happens in society and leaves one segment of it blind to the injustices it has for years been inflicting on another segment. And it happens in the use of Scripture far too often as we protect ourselves against those elements in Scripture which contradict our cherished convictions, our way of life, and our religious establishment. But where men stand before God their eyes are opened to the truth no matter how painful and distressing that truth may be. God is truth and to be open to his presence is to be receptive to the truth from whatever quarter it may appear. Honesty and integrity thus belong to the very essence of faith in God, and theology as the attempt to define the realities to which faith bears witness can live only in the atmosphere of unconditional truthfulness.

How serious, then, are the consequences for faith if Christians are something less than unconditionally honest in their dealings with Scripture! A little more than a century ago the novelist George Eliot, who had a keen if skeptical interest in theology, took the trouble to read through a number of books of sermons of a prominent evangelical preacher in London by the name of Dr. Cumming. She then published an essay on them which is still worth reading today.[38] What aggravated her in Dr. Cumming was his unwillingness to let the facts be the facts. He seemed to think that he needed to come to God's help with "little white lies." He had a theory about God's truth to which he had to make all the phenomena of Scripture conform. The church of today has in a great measure left the crudity and literalism of Dr. Cumming behind, but there is still frequently a protectiveness that surrounds the use of Scripture and a caution in the approach to its problems that is dangerously close to dishonesty. And just as honesty is the atmosphere in which truth thrives, so dishonesty is the atmosphere in which truth withers and dies and men become blind not just to what meets them in Scripture but to the realities of their own lives and of the society of which they are a part. Historical criticism, therefore, as it insists upon laying bare all that can be known concerning the text of Scripture, probing every problem to its depths, and disregarding what effect its findings may have for established traditions of the church, performs a highly important theological service to the church. It exposes both conscious and unconscious dishonesties in the church's interpretation of Scripture that rob the church's voice of its integrity, and it sets a standard of honesty that is bound to affect every aspect of the church's life. A church that is afraid to look into the Scriptures with open eyes lest it thereby lose something it considers essential to its life is not likely to have the courage or the faith to let its formulation of the gospel, its institutional existence, and the whole social order of which it is a part come under the really searching and disturbing scrutiny of the word of God that is to be heard at the heart of Scripture.

One achievement of historical criticism that was thought by some scholars to spell the end of all endeavors to find a unity in the theology of the Scriptures was the demonstration of the diversity that exists among the authors. As one of my teachers put it: "There are theologies of the Old Testament but no theology of the Old Testament." He would have said the same of the New Testament, and, of course, of the Bible as a whole. But this conclusion was, perhaps, a little hasty. There is a difference between unity and unanimity. Augustine, Thomas Aquinas, Luther, Calvin, and John Wesley have each of them a distinctive theology. There is no unanimity among them, but no one would dare to say that there is not unity. They belong together in a community of faith that is not destroyed but is enriched by the distinctive contri-

fifth contribution

bution of each. It would not have enhanced their unity
if they all had spoken with a single voice. So also with the
Biblical authors. When they were all pressed into a single
pattern and spoke with an enforced unanimity, violence
was done to the individual authors. Since the text was all
of it the direct utterance of deity, to find divergence or
contradiction in it was to posit a confusion of mind in God.
But it is a basic characteristic of men who stand before God
and bear witness to his truth that each in his own historical
situation speaks with an integrity that makes him a distinctive person who could never be confused with anyone
else. That is true both in the Scriptures and beyond the
Scriptures. Men who merely parrot someone else's words
bear witness thereby that they have never as yet stood alone
before God.

We do not have to expel Ecclesiastes from the Old Testament, then, because it speaks with a very different tone from
Second Isaiah, nor the letter of James because we doubt if
Paul would have approved its doctrine, nor the Gospel of
John because its description of Jesus' ministry fails to follow
the pattern common to the other Gospels. We can let each
author be himself and bear his witness in his own way. Amos,
Hosea, Isaiah, Jeremiah, Second Isaiah, and Ezekiel become
as real to us as men who lived only yesterday. We could no
more confuse the voice of Second Isaiah with that of eighth-
century Isaiah than we could mistake the poetry of Robert
Frost for that of William Wordsworth. Then there are those
powerful figures who have come out of the mists of the past
and taken definite form, each with his own theology, whom
we name so colorlessly J and P and D. In the New Testament,
where for a long time Paul and Peter were the only salient
figures apart from Jesus who appeared with any clarity, re-
dactional criticism is now making us familiar with the authors of each of the Gospels as distinctive theologians, giving
to each of them his own character. Also, the reconstruction
of early church history has brought the whole human scene

in the first-century church before us with a new clarity and in startling diversity from its first stages on. In the apostolic church there was certainly a unity but no theological unanimity. Unity and diversity were constantly in tension, sometimes explosive tension, with each other.

This penetration historically to the persons and situations behind the text has sometimes led to a so-called biographical approach to Scripture, as though this acquaintance with the persons provided us with the essence of Scripture and made close attention to their words superfluous. But we know the persons only in their words and our acquaintance with them as individual persons is valuable only as it enables us to hear more clearly what they say as they bear witness to the word that was their life. They become for us as we listen to them a wonderfully rich and diverse community of faith, prophets and apostles, psalmists and evangelists, with Jesus Christ at their center, and they invite us into their company. The goal of our Biblical studies becomes, not just that we may know and understand the text of Scripture, but that through the text this community of faith may become the primary context of our existence. Historical criticism helps to lay the very foundation of all our theology as it opens to us what is known in the creed as the communion of saints. That communion reaches far beyond the Scriptures. It spans the ages. But its fundamental rootage and the perennial source of its renewal is in the pages of the Scriptures, so that when the Scriptures lose their voice it begins to wither and die.

VII

The Reinterpretation of Authority

ONE FACTOR, as yet unconsidered by us, in the recession of the Scriptures in the life of the church and in the consciousness of Christian people has been the loss in authority that they have suffered increasingly in this century. How and why this has happened requires investigation, but the fact is indisputable. There was a time, not so long past, when a preacher had only to base his statements squarely on some part of the Biblical text to have them accepted unquestioningly by the majority of his hearers. The Biblical basis was taken to guarantee the truth of the utterance. But that time is past or is swiftly passing. No one should take comfort from the fact that there are still areas in the church where the Bible has that kind of authority because where it persists it is usually dependent upon a naïveté that perpetuates a childish, unquestioning attitude. The advance of education and the coming of maturity puts an end always to the mentality in which people are kept in the status of children, not thinking for themselves but obeying an external authority unhesitatingly. To expect the Bible to recover its authority through a renewal of such naïveté among Christians is not only futile but definitely unchristian, since it exalts the childish above the mature mind. We have no difficulty in recognizing that the pope is fighting a hopeless battle today as he tries to keep Catholics obedient children in relation to his authority. His people have come of age and are going to

[handwritten margin note:] this is puzzling, it seems to me, granted the pew-person's limited knowledge of the historical-critical method. It seems to me that an historical-critical interpreter would be less likely to accept something "because the bible says so" than a person who had no knowledge of, or had rejected, the historical-critical method.

"coming of age"

think for themselves whether he likes it or not. Equally evident is the folly of Moscow in demanding a similar obedience from the Communists of Czechoslovakia. Neither Communists nor Christians can remain forever children. Moreover, that Christians should want to think for themselves and make their own decisions rather than submit unquestioningly to an external authority is a sign not of their rejection of the Christian faith but of their maturing in it. What Protestants may be slow to recognize, however, is that childishly naïve submission to the Scriptures is of a piece with childishly naïve submission to the pope. The attitudes are directly parallel and in both we must recognize an unbiblical and theologically untenable concept of how God exercises his authority. It is not in the nature of God's authority to keep the members of his family perpetually in the role of children subject to a tutor, but rather the opposite, to make them stand on their own feet in his presence and in their relations with their fellowmen and face with open eyes the alternatives of life.

yes !!

When we inquire into the Bible's loss of authority in the modern world, we find a variety of factors at work. The first, as we have already seen, is modern man's refusal to remain a child, what Dietrich Bonhoeffer has taught us to call "man's coming of age." This is sometimes misunderstood as though it were a sweeping generalization about the whole human race, claiming that we have entered a new age in which all men in some mysterious way have suddenly reached maturity and are capable of managing their own lives without help or direction from any source beyond themselves. But that is closer to the superficial individualistic rationalism that Harry Overstreet[39] identifies with maturity than to Bonhoeffer's intention. It ministers to man's pride rather than to the clarity of his self-understanding. The Christian has to confess that shut in upon himself alone he finds how blind and helpless he is. His maturity is not a self-sufficiency. The sense in which his generation has come

the first factor in bibles loss of authority

of age and is mature is that it is unwilling any longer to trust itself blindly to *any* human guide, however venerable or endowed with divine unction that guide may be. The day of blind, unthinking obedience in religion, or in politics, or in education is past. Whether it be the church, the state, the university, or the home that is concerned, it must reckon with this insistence of men that they should participate in decisions in which their own existence is involved. All existing authorities are set in question by this development and the ferment of change in many different institutions is a product.

The authority of Scripture comes particularly into question because blind obedience to it has only too often in the past been used to fasten upon people attitudes that eventually turned out to be unchristian. Two centuries ago New Englanders on the authority of the Bible demanded and secured the execution of deranged old women who had been labeled witches by their neighbors. A century ago in another part of the land it was orthodox doctrine, based ostensibly on Scripture, that persons with a black skin must in all perpetuity be subordinated to persons who were fortunate enough to have been born with a white skin. But, closer still to our own time, there have been too many instances of men using the Scriptures in a highly selective fashion in order to secure conformity with their own particular interests, attitudes, and outlook for us to meet blanket assertions of its authority with anything other than skepticism.

A second factor has been the advance of modern knowledge which has done much to undermine the traditional authority of the Bible. The exploration of cultures and religions other than our own has shown a fair measure of wisdom distributed among all of them. No nation has had truth or goodness for its private preserve. Therefore an Israel that claims an exclusive role as witness to the one true God or a Christian church that regards itself as the sole repository and guarantee of divine truth seems to exhibit a narrowness of mind that is

second factor

I would argue that the bible's loss of authority is inevitable to a full-blown historical-critical criteria.

no longer tolerable. Then, from another angle, men who are conscious of how far the advances of the past century in science and in every sphere of knowledge have left the ancient and the medieval world behind find it absurd to attribute a unique and absolute authority regarding truth to a book whose latest writings were composed nearly nineteen centuries ago. The fact that until recently Christians in the Western world with their Bible regarded themselves as dwelling in the full radiance of truth while the remainder of humanity, beyond the borders of Christian civilization, was engulfed in an impenetrable darkness seems to them nothing less than scandalous. The tragic brutalities of the so-called Christian nations in the twentieth century and an enlarged acquaintance with such modern products of the "pagan" East as Gandhi and Nehru have made such cultural and religious egotism untenable. At the same time a more strictly honest portrayal of the history of the church has shown how often those who claimed exclusive possession of the truth shared the common human predicament of having their truth liberally mixed with error. None of these developments can be lightly brushed aside when we speak of the authority of Scripture if we hope to be convincing. Intellectually and actually we stand in a new situation and unless we can interpret that authority in such a way as to clear it of the charge of being a product of religious egotism and narrowness of vision, both in Israel and in the Christian church, we are not likely to persuade modern men that the Scriptures possess an authority for them which they must respect.

A third factor in the situation has, of course, been historical criticism. Conservatives have frequently been guilty of the error of holding historical criticism solely responsible for the eroding of the Bible's authority. They have ignored the first two factors and have spoken as though the entire problem would be solved if only the historical critics could be discredited. On the other hand, the error of Biblical scholars

[handwritten margin notes:] is this a possible task, given the rest of the author's argument.

factor #3

perhaps the bible is, in fact, largely a product of religious egoism; and maybe that's an unpleasant truth we must recognize

has been to minimize and so to obscure the devastating effect that their researches were bound to have upon the church's attitude to Scripture. Insofar as any view of authority depended upon an inerrant text, it was doomed from the beginning. Even an elementary comparison of the earliest Greek and Hebrew texts revealed a host of variant readings. But that disturbed only the most conservative churchmen. More significant and disturbing was the reconstruction of the history of Biblical times which sets in question the account of the history as it appears on the surface of Scripture. Add to this the disclosure of the long and complex development of religious ideas and practices that took place within the period covered by the Bible, Israelite religion giving way to Judaism and Judaism to Christianity. It becomes increasingly difficult to say what it is in the Scriptures that is still authoritative for modern man. The Old Testament, as it became the record of the more elementary stages of religious development preceding the appearance of the Christian religion with Jesus, suffered a severe depreciation in authority or lost it altogether. But historical research demonstrates the time-conditioned character of everything in the New Testament just as thoroughly, and, when it has finished its work, leaves man in a dilemma where to find the element in either Old or New Testament that is still authoritative for him. It is significant that when that most thorough historical scholar, Bultmann, has completed his analysis of the New Testament, he places the point of decisive authority not anywhere in the time-conditioned text but beyond the text in an indefinable kerygma.

C. H. Dodd, in his *The Authority of the Bible*,[40] offers a different solution. He, too, is aware that the text of Scripture is time-conditioned in every detail, but behind the text he finds a succession of religious geniuses, men who by their superior sensitivity to spiritual realities have seen more deeply into the meaning of life than their fellowmen. Their awareness of moral and spiritual values, their insights into the prob-

Dodd's solution

lems of humanity, the nobility of their ideas of God and man, equip them to be perennial guides to the rest of mankind. For Jesus, Dodd provided a special category. He was unwilling to call him only a religious genius and reverted to the traditional terms "incarnate word" and "human channel of the divine revelation," but the prophets and apostles with their merely "human insight" were thereby denied the authority that they claimed for themselves, of being divinely chosen servants of the same word that was incarnate in Jesus Christ. Dodd was falling between two stools. He was abandoning the concept of divine revelation for the text of Scripture as a whole but attempting to retain it for the person of Jesus. What he sought was a rationale for Biblical authority that could be established and demonstrated by the historian, that is, within the human, historical phenomena laid bare by historical research. But for Dodd the project broke down when he had to find a place at the center of it for Jesus Christ and in a later writing[41] he definitely abandoned the category of religious genius for prophets and apostles. He perhaps realized that "religious genius" is a vague and comprehensive term that not only dissolves the canon of Scripture but calls for a "Bible of the world" that embraces all religious geniuses. Augustine, Francis of Assisi, Luther, Confucius, Buddha, Gandhi, and a host of others clamor for inclusion. And, Jesus being set apart from his context in the prophets and apostles, in Israel and the church, it soon becomes meaningless to call him "the incarnate word." He, too, for the impartial historian, has to be given his place among the religious geniuses.

Dodd's reconstruction, therefore, did nothing to solve the church's problem. The point at issue is not whether there are unusual religious insights and values in the Scriptures. Anyone with an eye to see what is humanly important can see that there are. The Bible is a perfect mine of such insights and values. But what we want to know is whether or not the church is justified in setting this book apart from all

serygma. "

other books, even from those which are richest in similar insights and values, and in claiming that in it the truth concerning God and man and the meaning of life is revealed as it is nowhere else. To that issue the historian seems to have nothing very important to say, except to demonstrate that it is beyond the scope of his research. When he has done his best to define for us the content of Scripture, the question of authority is left hanging in the air.

*John
Bright*

John Bright's recent volume, *The Authority of the Old Testament*,[42] while it shares with Krister Stendahl the determination to maintain the character of Biblical scholarship as a purely objective descriptive science[43] and is confident that it can define not only the historical but also the theological content of the text with reasonable finality, nevertheless marks a distinct advance in the understanding of the Bible's authority. Bright takes full account of the effect of historical exegesis in accentuating the gulf between the text and the modern world. "To read the Old Testament in its literal meaning is to see it in its strangeness; and to see it in its strangeness is to raise again the question of Marcion," [44] that is, the question whether the Old Testament has any Christian significance. The literal meaning, arrived at by the grammatical-historical method, i.e., "the text taken as meaning what its words most plainly mean in the light of the situation to which they were originally addressed; the grammar interpreted against the background of 'history,' " [45] must control the entire interpretation, but of itself it is only the first stage in interpretation and leaves the text silent for those who live beyond that original situation. Bright pays tribute to Wilhelm Vischer[46] for forcing the Old Testament exegete to move on from a purely historical exegesis to a historical-theological interpretation. "Vischer certainly deserves our thanks for being among the first to remind us that we cannot rest content with a purely historical understanding of the Old Testament but must press on to see it in its Christian significance." [47] The text, therefore, once its literal meaning has been established, is to be set in its larger context, first of Old Testament theology as a whole and then of New Testament theology, in which the Old Testament reached its culmination. The theological context brings to light the theological content of the text that was obscured when it was heard only in its immediate historical context. Bright makes the claim that when this is done with *any* text of Scripture, not just specially selected texts but even the seemingly most unpromising texts, they take on a profound Christian significance for the present day, speak with a unique divine authority, and claim their traditional place of precedence in the preaching of the church. Old and New Testament theology, therefore, provide this larger context for interpretation.

Plausible

Bright has a curious explanation of the rebirth of interest in Old Testament theology. He attributes it to the archaeologists' forcing a revision of Wellhausen's pentateuchal theories and demonstrating that "Israel's religion did not evolve slowly from lower forms to higher but had already in all essentials assumed its normative form in the earliest period of Israel's life as a people." [48] It is unfortunate that the validity of Old Testament theology should be made dependent in any way upon the Albright reconstruction of the patriarchal age and also that the archaeologists rather than the theologians should receive the credit for reviving Biblical theology. But the most critical weakness of Bright's approach is his seeming unconsciousness of the importance of his own, or anyone's, interpretative context. Biblical theology, like historical exegesis, is for him a descriptive science, "an inductive, descriptive discipline that seeks through an examination of the Biblical records to determine and set forth in its own terms the essential and normative content of the faith of the Old Testament and the New respectively, as distinct from other faiths and as distinct from transient, peripheral, aberrant and incidental features within their own structure." [49] But what kind of a theological· content did this descriptive science find in the Old Testament fifty years ago, or even less than forty years ago? Were the scholars less scientific in the years when they were prepared to abandon the term "theology" and revelation for them was a mythological term for human insight? What actually were the events in the Christian world that impelled both Old and New Testament scholars to delve anew into the theological depths of Scripture? Certainly Bright has hold of the essence of the matter when he asserts that "there are no nontheological texts in the Bible," [50] and that "it is through its theology, not its ancient forms and institutions, that the Old Testament speaks with relevance and authority to the church," [51] but his Biblical theology is in danger, on the basis which he proposes, of becoming no more than a description of a complex of Biblical ideas and beliefs. If it is more than that for him—and plainly it is—is it the result wholly of his descriptive science, so that even an atheist using the same methodology could arrive at the same description of the theology, or has a special interpretative context played a part in the process? It is at this point that there needs to be some clarification.

Much of the difficulty that surrounds this problem of authority has arisen from the attempt of churchmen to make God's authority visible, tangible, and incontestable in a way that it never was for prophets or apostles or for Jesus himself. The authority of God's word everywhere in Scripture is invisible, intangible, and contestable. For those who experienced it, the authority was overwhelming. All human authorities became secondary and relative or were silenced before it. But when it was questioned, neither a prophet, nor an apostle, nor Jesus, could establish its validity in a rational and objective fashion. Jeremiah bowed before the authority of the word that sounded in his ears and called him into its service. When he tried to resist it and vowed that he would no longer serve it, it was like fire in his bones and he had to speak though the speaking might carry him to his ruin. But he had no way of proving to his fellow Judeans that his word was in truth the word of God himself. They could know its authority only by listening as he had listened, with his whole existence open toward God. The apostle Paul knew what it was to have his gospel and his apostolic authority challenged. He was accused of misleading Christians and misrepresenting Christ to the world. And what made the accusation especially painful was that it came from Christians who claimed to have on their side other apostles who had known Jesus in his earthly life. To many, that seemed to establish an imposing chain of external authority before which Paul was in a hopelessly weak position. But he made no attempt to establish for himself any comparable external authority. Rather he based his apostleship and his relationship to the church at large upon God's revelation to him, and through him, of the risen Lord. What Jeremiah knew as a fire in his bones Paul knew as an invisible, intangible presence by whose grace and under whose rule the life of the new age was reality for him and through him became reality for other men.

This hidden character of divine authority is evident also at the center of Scripture in the life and ministry of Jesus. Jesus spoke and acted with authority, an authority that angered the religious officials of his day who claimed for themselves an incontestable divine authority based securely upon the text of Scripture which they identified in every detail with the word of God. Jesus, in cleansing the Temple, had acted as though *he* were to be obeyed rather than the Temple officials. Then, each day as he taught in the Temple court he undoubtedly set in question, not directly but by implication, the whole established order of religion. Therefore the religious leaders came to him and asked him by what authority he acted as he did (Luke, ch. 20). The nature of his authority is evident in his answer. He refused to offer any explanation or proof of its validity. Instead, he asked his opponents a question to test their ability to recognize divine authority. A genuine prophet of God, John the Baptist, had recently been in their midst. Neither in his actions nor in his preaching had he conformed to any of the existing patterns of religion in Judaism. He had been sharply critical of the whole established order. His insistence upon all Israelites undergoing a baptism of repentance had been embarrassing and distasteful to a complacent religious community. Therefore Jesus' question, "Was John's baptism of divine or of merely human authority?" had a razor edge to it. John was a man sent from God to Israel, and, if these men could not recognize the integrity of his mission, then they would be unable to recognize any man sent from God, be his name John or Jeremiah or Moses or Jesus. They were unable to answer Jesus and, when they refused to answer, Jesus refused to discuss with them the nature of his authority. Jesus' authority was hidden except to faith. It was invisible, intangible, and contestable.

The Fourth Gospel is dominated by the consciousness of this hiddenness of God's authority in his Word. The word was present through the centuries in Israel but remained largely rejected and unknown. But wherever it found entrance and a welcome, men were born of God and knew themselves children of God. (John 1:11-12.) So also in the ministry of Jesus and in his death and resurrection, the Word that was incarnate in him was hidden from the eyes and minds of men until in it and in him they were willing to receive God himself in his Spirit and to come under the sovereignty of the Spirit. The Word and the Spirit are inseparable, which is just another way of saying that the word of God is not a series of words, ideas, beliefs or propositions, but is God himself in his chosen way of coming to man, and no one has heard God's word until in the hearing of the word he has received God himself in his Spirit to be the sovereign center of his existence and the wellspring of his life. To receive God's word is to know his sovereignty and therefore his authority.

invokes the "invisible, intangible and contestable" nature of biblical authority.

This, then, being the nature of God's authority for the prophets, for Jesus and for the apostles, it would seem to be axiomatic for a Christian church that it can assert for the Scriptures or for itself as their interpreter no other authority than was claimed by those primary witnesses. Yet again and again in history churchmen have in various ways tried to assert an authority that will be visible, tangible, and incontestable. It need not take the irrational form of attempting to maintain an inerrancy in Scripture. It is present also in Dodd's attempt to provide a rational, historical demonstration of the rootage of the authority in religious genius and even in some measure in Bright's claim by a purely inductive discipline to establish an objective Biblical theology that restores authority to the text of Scripture. The most impressive feature of Bright's book is his exposition of selected texts in which he sets them in their historical context and then goes on to let them be heard in their full theological context. It is in the exposition of the text that the Bible recovers its authority. It has to be laid open in its meaning for life now, whether in print, sermon, group discussion, or private conversation. The content of the text, freed from its time-conditioned context, and given a new contemporary clothing in which to meet the present human situation, asserts its own authority. It requires the services of the scholar and the interpreter to find its liberty but neither of them can ever, however much he tries, make its authority other than invisible, intangible, and contestable.

like Bultmann, you are searching for anything to grasp on to, Mr. Smart. And, like Bultmann, you resort to obscurantism.

can one mesh "contestable" with "authority?" Is it really fair — is it not just getting yourself off the hook — to say, Well, there's something secret or hidden about biblical authority. I would contend that something "hidden" cannot be "authoritative"

VIII

The Relation Between History
and Revelation

OUR CONSIDERATION of the nature of Biblical authority
brings us to the verge of one of the most controversial
subjects in Biblical interpretation. The most eminent scholars
are divided not just into two camps but into the widest diversity concerning the relation between history and revelation in the Scriptures. We have already at a number of points
seen the limitation of historical science that, when it has
laid out before us in scrupulous detail all the phenomena of
Biblical literature, history, and religion, and even when it
has presented most sympathetically the salient figures—
patriarchs, prophets, Jesus, and Paul—though we may be
impressed by the wisdom, moral courage, and spiritual insight that are demonstrable, we find ourselves still without
justification in setting these writings apart from all other
literature in which wisdom, moral courage, and spiritual
insight are present. The authority which, over a period of
a thousand years, a series of men claimed for their utterances,
and which the traditions that preserved the memory of
those utterances and of actions associated with them continue
to claim, was nothing less than the authority of God himself.
Both then and now that claim has been exposed to the acids
of human skepticism, and all the more so when those
who make the claim are found, first in Israel and then in the
early Christian church, asserting the absolute uniqueness of
God's revelation of himself to them. The prophet saw Israel

as a nation chosen from among all the nations of the world as witness in word and life to the reality of the one true God, not exalted above the other nations by the word of truth entrusted to it but made the servant of all in being the servant of the word.[52] So also, the early Christians were certain that the knowledge of God which in Jesus had set them in the dawn of a new age for humanity was accessible through him alone, attributing to him the words, "No man cometh unto the Father except by me" (John 14:6). The decision whether or not this seemingly outrageous claim is valid is not within the competence of historical science but calls rather for the theologian whose understanding of reality does not limit it to human and historical phenomena but finds, in the human and historical, evidence of an underlying relationship between God and man.

The claim of prophets and apostles is that there has been entrusted to them a knowledge of God in which man comes to the only true understanding of himself, his neighbor, and his world. For Hosea this knowledge is the very foundation of a nation's life and the neglect of it by prophets and priests brings in its train a blindness and corruption in social and political life. (Hos. 4:6; 6:6.) For Paul it is the source of an infinite blessedness, a light that must eventually overcome all darkness. But it is a special kind of knowing, a knowing and being known in a personal relationship in which the total being of a man is comprehended and not just his intellect. The content of the knowledge cannot be set down in propositions because the relationship with God in which it has its reality is of a dimension that refuses ever to be bound by man's definitions and persistently breaks through every formula that he devises to describe it. The distance between God's thoughts and man's best thoughts is of the essence of the relation. (Isa. 55:8-9.) The prophet describes this knowledge as a word that God has hidden in Israel. The prophet may hear it more clearly than others, but it is planted like a seed deep in the life of the nation and the

history of the nation is determined by it from beginning to
end, whether the response be obedience or disobedience.
The word is God's way of being with man in the midst
of his history. So also the history of the New Israel, the
church, is determined by the Incarnate Word which is im-
planted in it at the moment of its birth. It is this word, this
knowledge, this continuing relationship of God with men,
that we are trying to describe when we speak of revelation.
The history is incomprehensible apart from it; the history
bears witness to it as a presence and power breaking into it
that sets it in motion, and yet it so transcends the history
that it can never be reckoned merely an element in the
history.

possibility of misunderstanding

When we call this knowledge that is at the heart of the
history of both Israel and the church "revelation" we introduce possibilities of serious misunderstanding. The attention
tends to be focused on special visions and auditions, and
revelation is identified with such occasional experiences
rather than with the less spectacular but constant awareness
of the source of life's meaning and direction in the Beyond,
the Beyond which is ever present and inescapable. Revelation thus becomes a peculiarity of Biblical times that one
does not expect to find present in his own life experience.
The revealing took place *then* and resulted in a Bible that
preserves for us what was *then* revealed. Thus the content of
the Bible is identified with the content of the revelation, for
the literalist the content of the Bible as a whole, but for
many others who have left literalism behind, the theological
content of the Bible that can be codified as doctrines and
beliefs. But this negates the primary nature of revelation as
it is defined for us by Scripture itself. Revelation is God's
presence with man in the midst of his history, illumining
his life situation, setting him free from his past, and opening before him a new future. It leaves its marks upon the
history. Men bear witness to the presence they have known,
and, whether they respond in praise and thanksgiving or

in revolt and angry rejection, their response is witness to a confrontation with something more than just their fellowman. The Bible is therefore witness to revelation, to a revelation, however, that is reality *only* in actual history, so that the Bible must not ever be equated with the revelation itself.

The crucial testimony of the early church in the New Testament is not just that the hopes of Israel were fulfilled in Jesus Christ but that all human history reached its goal when in him God and man were at one, and the long, painful contradiction between God and man was overcome. In him a new humanity was born and a new age in history began. God with man is therefore a historical existence, whether it be in ancient Israel, in the person of Jesus, in the apostolic church, or in man's life today. But it is a form of historical existence that historical science cannot grasp in its full and living reality without flattening it out into a complex of man's experiences and ideas of God or into a stage in man's self-understanding.[53] The Scriptures are more reverent and realistic. They preserve the mystery of the relation of man with the unseen. They are content simply to be witness to the unique relation between God and Israel and the unique presence and action of God in Jesus Christ and in his church. But when they find men open and receptive to their witness, they become the means whereby God's presence in judgment and promise and the new humanity and the new age that dawned in Jesus Christ begin to dawn upon us with the same freshness and excitement. *Revelation is the actuality of God with man.* It is judgment. It is a transforming pardon. It is grace. It is new life. It is joy in the Holy Spirit. It is the opening of our eyes to the truth about ourselves and our fellowmen. It is the sensitizing of our consciences to the injustice and cruelty and lovelessness that deface our human existence. It is the abolition of the barriers between man and man that our blindness has created. There is no revelation merely in a book. Revelation is God coming to man and God is not willing to be locked up between the covers of a book. God's presence is not in a book but is with man. The risen Lord is not in a book but in the midst of his people. And yet the Bible is indispensable if we are to know God and if we are to be in truth the body of the risen Lord, because through it alone are we able to listen with Israel and with the apostolic church for the unique word out of the unseen which was for them, and can be for us, the power of God bringing our human life to its fulfillment.

It is evident, then, that revelation is intimately involved with history, that is, with man's life in time. The relationship with God calls for a distinctive relationship of man with man and it sets up a profound tension between man's life as it is and man's life according to God's intention. The very reality of history as a movement of man's life toward a goal is born of this tension. Revelation creates history. Revelation in the Old Testament is God unfolding his purpose for man's historical existence, and revelation in the New Testament is God taking decisive action in Jesus Christ and in his church to overcome the destructive forces in human history and to create a new world. Therefore any separation of revelation from history or of history from revelation leads to a complete misunderstanding of both. They must be held together in the unity that they have in Scripture.

At this point a major difficulty has arisen in the modern interpretation of Scripture. Part of the difficulty lies in the variety of meanings that are placed on the two words "history and "revelation" and the different ways in which their relation to each other is understood. James Barr[54] finds so much confusion at this point among scholars that he would like to abandon the word "revelation" (though not the reality signified by it) and define with more discrimination just what it is in the historical phenomena that God uses to fulfill his purpose with us. His major criticism is directed against G. Ernest Wright's overly facile identification of *heilsgeschichte*

revelation with "acts of God in history," [55] which fails to do justice to the significance of revelation in "word" and to the complexity of Israel's tradition. Barr rightly emphasizes the variety of elements that play a part in Israel's witness to revelation but, because of his failure to identify the substance of the revelation as a unique life sustained in the community by its relation with God, the unity of the elements eludes him and he leaves the problem still in confusion. How great the present confusion is becomes evident when we list the varying viewpoints of prominent theologians. Oscar Cullmann,[56] like Wright, focuses upon "acts of God in history," which in their continuity form a "salvation history" and disclose the plan and purpose of God in all history. The identification of revelation with this "salvation history" which is directly accessible to the historian fails to do justice to the hiddenness of God's self-revelation or to the distinction between God's action and the visible consequences of his action. Wolfhart Pannenberg[57] widens the scope of the history that is to be identified with revelation to take in all history from its beginning to its end, but qualifies the word "history" to mean not history in the raw but "interpreted history" since no event is accessible to any man except in a context of interpretation. For Rudolf Bultmann, however, revelation is wholly from beyond history, though sometimes this seems to mean from an "inside" of history that is accessible to those who let themselves become existentially involved. Karl Barth would agree with Bultmann that God's action in history is hidden and inaccessible to the historian and, like him, would insist that it is *in* history though at a depth that conceals it except from the eyes of faith. To describe this level of reality which is *in* history yet not accessible to the historian he coined the term *"Urgeschichte,"* which may be translated "primal history." In distinction from Bultmann, however, he asserts that God's action leaves its marks upon the visible history to constitute a "salvation history," which is not itself revelation but only witness to it. R. R. Niebuhr[58] rep-

views points of various scholars

resents still another viewpoint in his recognition of the resurrection of Jesus in its significance for revelation as the crucial event of all history which requires of the historian that he reconsider his definition of what constitutes history. This variety of convictions and their obviously contradictory character warn us that this area in hermeneutics is drastically in need of clarification and that we should venture upon it with caution as onto a battleground.

It may help to clarify what is at issue if we think for a moment not of history in the large, Biblical history or world history, but in the smaller region of our own personal experience. Each of us has lived a portion of history and has the body of it available in his memory. Let us suppose that after your death a historian decided to write an account of your life. He would assemble all available evidence, information about your ancestors in whom your life was already taking some of its shape, childhood influences, educational developments, your friendships, how you found your vocation, the crises you surmounted, the tasks you undertook, and what you made of them. But how easy it would be for him to miss the inner core of the story which is the dialogue with God (only infrequently formulated in words) which has been there from as far back as you can remember. He would catch glimpses of it here and there, but the most important moments in that dialogue have been hidden from every human eye and have left no record except in their outward consequences. We are all of us like icebergs which show only a small portion of themselves above the surface and whose deeper regions remain invisible, in some measure hidden even from ourselves. But the invisible and the visible are both essential to the history. And would we not say that often what God was doing with us in the visible events was hidden from us at the time and only later came to recognition as we interpreted them in the larger context of God's total dialogue with us in time? God has been the primary, creative, determinative factor in our history, but

there is no such thing as dialogue with God, only monologue, for God never speaks

the historian would find it difficult to get farther in his explorations than a fragmentary account of our experiences and ideas of God. He would incorporate the divine factor in his description of our religion. He might even question whether what we called "God" was anything more than a projection of our own consciousness if his theological inclinations were toward skepticism. But if he were an open-minded historian, he would at least leave room in his portrayal for the possibility that our dialogue with God really constituted the core of our history and was not merely a mythological interpretation, which all our life we had been reading into the events.

What we recognize at once when we see it in relation to our own remembered experience is that the observations of even the most competent historian are limited. His methodology enables him to reconstruct the complex of past events and to penetrate the thoughts and experiences of men which have shaped the character of the events, but its competence diminishes as it moves from the visible and the tangible level where there is concrete evidence and attempts to take account of the deeper, hidden levels of man's past existence. The temptation of the historian has always been to think that what he has been able to reconstruct is the whole story of the past and our temptation in reading history is to regard the visible and the tangible as possessing a reality that we withhold from the less visible and tangible elements in the past. But from our own experience we know that the most real factors in our existence are hidden from the eye of any observer and that what is visible and tangible can never be rightly understood unless account is taken of those deeper levels at which our life is shaped.

This consideration brings to light our embarrassment in the English language at having only the one word "history" to describe two quite different but closely related entities. Because the same word has to be used for both, we constantly lose sight of the important and vital distinction between

the two kinds of history

them. The Germans are fortunate in having two words to use. For the total reality of the past as a stream of life that has visible and invisible levels they use the word *Geschichte*, and for the reconstruction of the past that has been produced by historical science they use the word *Historie*.[59] This holds the two apart and makes it easier to remember that what the historian produces as history in his reconstruction is not the whole reality of the past but only the more visible and tangible aspects of it which have been accessible to his methodology. The importance of this distinction is driven home when we see how in the first few decades of the twentieth century a dominant historicism, blind to its limitations, came close to reducing God to one of man's nobler ideas and the Bible to little more than a chapter in the story of man's religion.

We must not let ourselves be carried, however, from a recognition of the historian's limitations to a depreciation of the importance of his ruthlessly critical methodology. We should have no quarrel with him, nor should we accuse him of skepticism when in dealing with the Biblical record he confines himself to what is humanly describable. It is inevitable that the history of Old and New Testament times which he presents will be shockingly different from the story as the Biblical authors themselves portray it. In the Biblical account human and divine actions are mingled together, but the modern historian in the integrity of his science can tell only the human story. All we can ask of him is that he leave the door open to the credibility of divine action in history. He can give us only a fragmentary account of Jesus' historical life when his critical analysis of the Gospels is finished, and we feel the sharpness of the contrast with the full, rich story as we have it in the Biblical text. The Incarnate Lord, the divine Savior, the atoning death, the resurrection triumph are no longer there. But we should know that they cannot be there for the scientific, objective historian since they belong to that hidden level of reality that is not accessible to outward observation. So also his reconstruction of the early church presents a different picture from what is given us in The Acts. But that need not trouble us. The Acts of the Apostles is testimony to the continued presence and power of the risen Lord in the midst of his church, forcing it out of the narrow confines of Palestine to embark on a mission to the whole world. It draws aside the curtain to show *God* at work in the activities of men. The historian, however, has to leave the curtain between man and God in place. His task, a very important task, is to reconstruct as accurately as possible the human scene and the human story.

It is unfortunate that at several points in his *Church Dogmatics* Karl Barth has seemed to deprecate this work of the Biblical historian when he condemns the attempt to go behind the Biblical text in order to reconstruct what actually happened.[60] He considered it futile to try to piece together the fragments of a historical life of Jesus when the only Jesus remembered by the early Christians was the Christ of God who in his ministry, death, resurrection, and living presence was the fulfillment of all the promises of God to man. It is unfortunate because Barth himself is a historian of unusual competence and one would expect him to recognize that no area of the past can be exempted from critical historical investigation, and certainly not the area of Biblical history, whether it has to do with the life of David or the life of Jesus. But, having said that, one has to appreciate Barth's concern at this point to warn men against thinking that the historian can present to us either the story of Israel or the story of Jesus that is most significant for us as a Christian church. It is the Israel of the Old Testament whose whole existence was determined, positively or negatively, by its personal relation with God, by what we might call its controversy with God, and the Christ of the New Testament who is so at one with the Father that in confrontation with him men are face to face with God himself whether they know it or not, who command the primary interest and concern of the church. Barth is right that, if we think by going behind the New Testament text to a reconstructed Jesus of history, we shall lay hold on a solider reality than the Christ of faith or the risen Lord, we are the victims of a serious illusion. The Jesus of history is an abstraction from the *larger* reality remembered and known in the early Christian community. So also, the traditions embodied in the Old Testament are witness to a centuries-long dialogue of God with Israel and of Israel with God which was the very essence of Israel's existence and yet which tends to get lost from sight in the historian's reconstruction of those centuries. It seems, therefore, that what Barth was trying to say was that the Biblical text as we have it, just because it mingles the divine and human elements in the story, presents to us the whole reality of Israel and the whole reality of Jesus Christ in a way that no reconstructed history of Israel or of Jesus can pretend to do.

Nowhere do the different aspects of this problem appear more clearly than in the account of Jesus' death and resurrection. For the Christian church these two events which are actually inseparable have been the climactic point in the whole story of God's revealing of his heart and mind to man and, as a consequence, the decisive turning point in human history, the point at which a new age began. The story as it comes to us from the early church is a mixture of history and theology with the two so intertwined that to separate them is to produce a different story from any that was ever told by the disciples of Jesus. Yet a descriptive historical science is forced to separate the history from the theology, isolating first the historical event and then the meaning that the church found in the event. The crucifixion of Jesus, one of the most firmly and vividly attested events in history, can be understood quite adequately from the interplay of forces that are evident in his mission. The course he adopted was a bold challenge to the established order in Judaism and his tone in controversy with his opponents did nothing to lessen the tension. Pre-Christian Paul, like many others, saw in him a threat to the future of the whole religious and social structure. If he was heralded as the messianic king, then that would make him a threat also to the Romans and would hasten his execution. At no point is it necessary to posit any action of God in the event to explain the cross. Rather, history seems to say that here God did nothing, that the man Jesus was left completely at the mercy of grim historical forces. But finally the historian bumps up against the mystery why the church seized upon this tragic event, which actually had in it so many humiliating features, and made it the very core of its gospel, not, as one might have expected from the Old Testament background, as the story of a prophet's martyrdom but as the Redeemer's victory over all the powers of evil, death, and hell which hold mankind enslaved and blinded.

Why was it the death of *Jesus* that had this universal significance and not the deaths of earlier faithful prophetic witnesses? Why was God's redemptive action seen in the crucifixion of Jesus and not in the beheading of John the Baptist? Here the historian has to confess himself completely at a loss. He can report only what the early church made of the cross, calling it an interpretation of the historical event. He can affirm that Christians, contemplating the cross of Jesus, were moved to a remarkable self-abnegation and a courageous commitment of themselves to the extension of Jesus' mission. But he cannot as a historian either confirm or deny the claim of the first Christians that God was present and active in the event of the cross, bringing all human sin under judgment and reconciling a sinful humanity to himself. Actions of God are not accessible to the objective historian. But if he argues that because they are not accessible to him they are of doubtful reality, he is an incautious historian, expressing not a scientific historical judgment but an irresponsible negative theological judgment. He is denying reality to anything in the past that does not come within the scope of his observation.

This is even more evident when we consider the resurrection. Where the cross could almost be expected as the culmination of observable developments in the mission of Jesus, the resurrection of Jesus has no antecedent history. It is reported as a wholly unexpected event by the immediate disciples of Jesus, but it is clearly a strange kind of event which, although it had in it power to create in the disciples a triumphant faith, could be regarded as a hoax by interested contemporaries. The crucifixion on its surface level was open to observation by anyone who happened to be in Jerusalem, but not the resurrection. It had the character solely of a theophany, a revelation of God, except that it was a revelation of Jesus, the historical person whom the disciples had known, now revealed as they had not known him but as he truly was. To the disciples and Paul the resurrection was a confrontation with the Jesus who had been crucified, an experience in which the blindness was struck from their eyes and they saw him in his oneness with God, the Servant Lord of all humanity, triumphant over death. But the historian is unable to validate even the objectivity of the event. Its historicity is in question for him. He cannot see beyond the visionary experiences of the disciples and Paul, to which he must attribute an amazing significance in the generation of the gospel and the church, but which he may explain in a quite naturalistic fashion as the product of hysteria.[61] He is more comfortable, like Bultmann, to regard the resurrection of Jesus not as an event in the history of Jesus' relation with his disciples but as an event in the faith of the disciples as they died to their old selves and rose into their new life with God. But this view too is the product of a negative theological judgment that refuses to assert for Jesus a continuing presence and activity beyond his death except as a subjective element in the faith of his disciples.

What, then, are the implications of all this for hermeneutics and homiletics? First, we are warned not to expect of a descriptive historical science more than it is competent to achieve. Its task is to reconstruct for us as accurately as possible the full *human* story. But it cannot penetrate beyond human actions, experiences, and ideas to reconstruct the actuality of a relation of God with man. Nor should we let our definition of historical reality be dictated to us by the historian. The nature of historical reality is the nature of human and divine existence in their interrelation, a theological question to which every answer is either positively or negatively theological even when it comes from a secular historian. The Scriptures define historical reality as an unceasing dialogue between God and man, and the authority of that definition for us depends upon the ability of the Scriptures to illumine the dialogue with God which underlies our own present historical existence.

Second, we are made more sharply aware of what a fatal error it is to locate the authority of Scripture in what is visible, external, historical. Conservative and liberal alike have contributed to this error and thereby undermined the authority: the conservative by locating it in an infallible text and the liberal by locating it in the spiritual values, insights, ideas, and beliefs. Both are futile attempts to make God visible and God confutes them both by hiding himself. It is universally true that God is hidden except to faith. God protects himself against desecration by his hiddenness even in the person of Jesus. How then is the authority of Scripture to be reestablished? There is no other way than through the faithful preaching and teaching of the Scriptures and through the response of a people to that preaching and teaching whereby their life as a community becomes a living witness to God's presence and power.

Third, we must not let the valid emphasis upon hearing the text in its original historical context blind us to the importance of hearing the text in its full original theological context. The historical context sets the speaker or writer in relation to the human situation of his time. The theological context sets the speaker in his place in the ongoing dialogue between God and his people to which everything in Scripture is somehow related and which continues through all time. For descriptive historical science man's thoughts concerning God are primary, but for all our Biblical authors it is God's thoughts concerning man that are primary. We start from man to work up somehow to God, but they start from God to work down to man. We try to peer from the visible into the invisible, but they take their stand firmly with God in the unseen and from there look penetratingly into our human situation. The initiative is with God, and man's life in history is determined by the response he makes to God. But there is no depreciation of man's share in the dialogue. The Scriptures consist not just of God's words to man but also in a large measure of man's words, and an account of man's actions, in response to God. And the human response is as essential to us as the divine initiative. Both sides of the dialogue belong together. Even when the response is rebellion and disobedience it is rebellion and disobedience in the context of the total dialogue (which is merely another name for the covenant relation), and can have its share in bearing witness to the faithfulness and mercy of God. It is here that the rule "Scripture its own interpreter" is in place. The Scriptures as a whole, and in spite of the immense variety of religious viewpoints that are to be found within them, set before us the drama of God's dealings with man in history. It is the story of God's fashioning of man to be truly man and we see it in all its heights and depths, from its beginning to its end. Every element in Scripture has its ultimate meaning in the context of that story. And the moment when we come to know the authority of Scripture is when at some point or other we suddenly become aware that it is all of it *our* story, the story of *our* life, the story of God's fashioning of *us* and *our* world to be truly human.

IX

The Widening
of the Gap

IN AN EARLIER CHAPTER we saw what an important part is played by the interpretative context in which the Scriptures are read, and how, though everyone without exception reads them in such a context, the reader is rarely conscious of the character of the context, so that it has to be dredged up out of the unconscious if it is to be subjected to criticism. We need now to do a little dredging. It has become clear that one of the chief obstacles to the preacher in his preaching from the Scriptures and to his people in their hearing is that, whereas most preachers by their training in seminary have moved out of the precritical into the critical age of interpretation, their people have been left in the precritical age. The two no longer have the same interpretative context in their approach to Scripture. But the interpretative context is shaped by many other factors than what is heard in church. It is beyond the control of any ecclesiastical authority because it is exposed to all the winds of change that blow. Our minds are furnished from the earliest moments of consciousness by the age in which we live, and in the modern era of mass communication the child on the farm or in the village is as exposed to the spirit of the age as the one in the most advanced center of culture. We need not think, therefore, that the membership of the church has remained in a naïve, uncritical interpretative context waiting for a more courageous ecclesiastical leadership to take them out of it. The world of which they are a part has moved out of the precritical age in every other department of life and they have moved with it. It is chiefly in their religion that they have been allowed to lag behind. Most of them are quite aware of the tension between the mind they seem to be expected to wear in church and the mind to which they are accustomed in all the other situations of life. The spectacular response to Bishop Robinson's *Honest to God* was the result not so much of anything new in its theology but rather of his addressing himself, in language a layman can understand, to the questions the layman's mind is being forced to ask by the spirit of the age but which he fails to hear discussed in church. That a bishop should be saying what he thought about such questions without the caution usual in a bishop undoubtedly added spice for the layman.

In the last four hundred years vast changes have taken place that have revolutionized not just the outward structure of our world but also the inner furnishings of the mind. Luther had to break free of a medieval hermeneutic that was rooted in an antiquated order of both church and society in order to hear and deliver the message of the Scriptures to his own age. But in many respects Luther remained a child of the ancient world. The world of Luther and the world of the Bible had much in common in spite of the fifteen centuries intervening. One of the things that delighted Luther about the Old Testament was that so many of the scenes and situations in it were like a mirror in which he could see his own world reflected. The kings of Israel and Judah and the princes of the German states had much in common. The stories of demon possession and the expulsion of demons in the New Testament were not strange to him as they are to us, for he too inhabited a world infested with demons and on one occasion threw an inkwell at what he took to be the devil himself. His world like that of the Bible had three levels to it: the heaven above, the hell so danger-

concerning a new world view

ously close beneath men's feet, and the world of living men between. The story of creation had no problems for him since he still thought of the sun, moon, and stars as rotating round the earth as their center and pivot. The vastness of our universe and the relative tininess of our earth in the midst of it were unknown to him. Ernst Troeltsch was right in his insistence that in many aspects of their mentality the Reformers still belonged to the Middle Ages and that the modern age began not with them but with the Enlightment in the eighteenth century.

I agree

Karl Barth, in his *Die protestantische Theologie im 19. Jahrhundert*,[62] devotes almost the whole of the first two hundred pages to the eighteenth century in order to show that the questions that have occupied the theologians not only in the nineteenth but also in the twentieth century have been those which were posed already in the eighteenth century. Part of the church's problem is that the influence of the Enlightenment is only now reaching the broad membership of the church. Paul Hazard describes the change in France shortly after 1700 as dramatically sudden: "One day the French people, almost to a man, were thinking like Bossuet. The day after, they were thinking like Voltaire." [63] A whole new way of looking at the world and at oneself, of investigating every aspect of it, and of mastering its problems took over in the mind of Western man. The change may have been sudden and dramatic in France, but for most of the population of the Western world it has been so gradual as to be almost imperceptible. When we see it spelled out in detail in a book such as John Henry Randall's *The Making of the Modern Mind*,[64] it is a shock to us to realize that our mental world is so radically and comprehensively different from that of our ancestors. We did not realize that the gap between then and now could be so wide.

The rise of historical-critical scholarship was contemporary with the Enlightenment and a product of it. It was the result of men attempting to read the Scriptures with the same mind with which they were examining other historical documents and investigating other areas of man's existence. They were not willing to let either the Bible or their religion become merely fossils from an ancient world. That they met with passionate and abusive resistance is not surprising, for the sanction that faith lends to the truth on which it rests is frequently extended to the whole traditional context, which has come to be associated with the faith but which actually is not essential to it. Every man in order to function in the world builds up a kind of microcosm, a model of the world, in his own mind, which may or may not correspond closely with the actual world. It is the product not only of his direct impressions and all the information that has reached him but also of his interpretation, meditation, and imagination. And because it is the world in which he lives his inmost life, he may be slow to surrender any part of it. He feels his very existence threatened when called upon to change the structure of his microcosm and he may even feel it as a challenge to the existence of his God. Thus, some people persisted and still persist, at least in the religious lobe of their minds, in living in a Biblical-medieval world and in preserving the mentality of that world, but for most of us, and for these others perhaps more than they know, that is a lost cause. There is only one world and we condemn our words and actions to unreality and futility unless our microcosm, the world that exists in our imagination, is kept in closest correspondence with the actual world.

There are two ways in which in the past the church has tried to meet this problem—the one conservative and the other liberal—and both of them have been failures. The conservative response has been an attempt, to some degree at least, to preserve the mentality of that earlier age in order to narrow the gap between the Bible and the Bible reader. It is a pathetic operation. The six days of creation are defended against the millennia of the evolution of the universe, until finally even the State of Tennessee is forced to take *conservative approach*

its prohibition of the teaching of evolution off its statute books. The believers are expected to accept unquestioningly as history the report of every miracle in Scripture, even the axhead which Elisha made float for his brother prophet and the sun standing still in Aijalon, though similar miracles are not anticipated in the present world. The ascension is still pictured as a levitation from the Mount of Olives to a heaven that is just above the blue of the sky, though that positioning of heaven can be maintained only in a special religious atmosphere and not in a world where astronauts journey to the moon. These are extreme examples but representative of the preservation of an antique mentality. The official doctrine of Scripture for most Presbyterians throughout the world is one formulated in 1647 which commits them to a speculative inerrancy of the original manuscripts of both Testaments, speculative because the originals are lost beyond recovery. Although Presbyterian churches in general have moved away from such a doctrine, conservative influences have usually been strong enough to prevent an official reformulation of the doctrine in the light of the last three centuries of Biblical research—until the recent action of The United Presbyterian Church in the U.S.A. Not until 1967 did a Presbyterian church dare to free itself officially and legally from the mentality of the precritical age, and even then it had to contend with a fair amount of resistance!

The conservative ploy is to make the modern reader contemporary with the Scriptures, that is, to make him conform mentally to the thought world of the Biblical authors, rather than to let the Scriptures become contemporary with the modern reader. There is a real sense in which in good exegesis we do go back and enter the author's world, learning his language and letting him speak to us in his own peculiar thought forms. But we do not have to exchange our own twentieth-century language and thought forms for his in order to hear him speak any more than we would have to adopt the language and thought forms of a Chinese Buddhist in order to converse with him. To attempt to preserve the mentality of the seventeenth century or the first century or any preceding age is futile. In secular life the futility is very quickly demonstrated and the attempt is abandoned. But in the religious realm the futility is more easily concealed and the tensions that are produced are destructive.

the liberal approach

The liberal response to the problem has been a reductionist procedure, to make the Bible contemporary by excerpting from it those elements which seem to transcend every age and to have eternal value. Whatever is unacceptable to the modern mind, whatever is strange and alien, is allowed to fall away as unessential, leaving a precious residue of abiding truths. The task is to distinguish between what is time-conditioned and belongs only to the expression of faith in the Biblical era and what remains valid for the life of man through all the changes of time. A simple task it may seem at first, and a marvelous liberation. With one great sweep of the broom a mass of traditions both Biblical and confessional, in which the modern mind can find no relevance, is brushed aside. Miracles and a God who acts in history, a three-story universe and with it the doctrines of incarnation, resurrection, and ascension, the virgin birth and with it any attribution of divinity to Jesus, the canon of Scripture and the concept of revelation, all alike are categorized as temporary expressions of a faith that can be disengaged from them and reexpressed in terms that will offer no offense to any modern intelligence. Sooner or later, the suggestion was bound to be made that even the concept of God belonged to that ancient world which we have outgrown so that the really honest Christian should abandon it and reexpress his faith in purely human terms. And, in a world where in most areas of life the hypothesis of a God seems to have become unnecessary, the suggestion could be seriously entertained.

The liberal procedure turns out to be a capitulation of the Christian to the authority of the modern mind which lets the Bible become contemporary by letting most of it recede into a world so far away from us that we can no longer make contact with it at all. And then the suspicion arises inevitably that the precious essence extracted from it is actually more a congenial product of our own time than anything that the prophets, Jesus, or the apostles would have recognized as their own. It is doubtful if the prophets would have been persecuted or Jesus crucified for proclaiming with Harnack the fatherhood of God and the brotherhood of man. Bultmann's critique of liberalism went to the heart of the matter: the weakness of liberalism was a failure to recognize that *everything* in Scripture is a time-conditioned expression of faith from which no eternal essence can be extracted, that the essential message is to be discovered not beyond the time-conditioned expressions but in them, and that the message, when discovered, is marked not by a congeniality to the modern mind but by the way in which it challenges that mind to decision. Liberalism was much too uncritical of the modern mind and too ready to abandon whatever seemed to it unintelligible; the truth of Christ crucified and risen so cuts across the mind of every age and offends it that it has the semblance of nonsense. And, with its abandonment, Christianity becomes little more than a religious form of humanism.

When one considers how much of the church's practice in the twentieth century is comprehended in these two procedures, the conservative and the liberal, and how intrinsically both of them were doomed to failure, one begins to understand why the impression is widespread, not just outside the church but among people who have spent their lives inside the church, that it is futile to expect the Scriptures to have much in them that is contemporary.

Two other factors that have operated to widen the gap between the Bible and the man of today have both had to do

with history. The one has been the neglect of history, church
history and world history, in the church's educational
program, and the other the way in which for anyone interested in history the horizons have been pushed out in time
and space to a stupendous distance.

Until very recently it was not considered important in the
church's educational programs to spend time on the nearly
nineteen centuries of history that separate Bible times from
the present time. Attention was focused almost exclusively
on the Bible and on problems of Christian conduct, and,
in the haste to make the Biblical text relevant to modern life,
a minimum of attention was given even to the history of Old
and New Testament times. And yet, if the Bible is to speak to
us, it is essential that we establish not just continuity but a
very real identity between the world of the Bible and the
world in which we live day by day. We have to be able to
enter imaginatively into the events of Jesus' ministry and the
struggles of the early church in which our own church and
our own life as Christians was coming into being. It has to
become *our* story, more essential to our existence than the
immediate events of our family life. The neglect of Biblical and post-Biblical history, however, destroys the continuity
and allows the stage on which the Biblical drama is acted to
take on an atmosphere of unreality. This is encouraged from
an early age in the minds of children by the fact that they
hear Bible stories and fairy stories and the two intermingle.
What difference can they see between the magic wand that
turns a frog into a prince and the rod of Aaron that turns
itself into a snake at his command? Moses raises his hand
and the waters of the sea divide. Jesus or Peter have only to
speak a word and lame men are no longer lame. The Bible
world like the fairy world is full of good and evil spirits.
This similarity makes the Bible world all the more delightful
to the child, but the child is soon aware that the fairy world
is a never-never world and not the world in which he lives,
so that, with the intermingling of Bible world and fairy

world, the former becomes a never-never world. So persistent is that childhood experience that even mature scholars when first they visit Palestine have an eerie feeling in setting foot upon that soil and finding it firm beneath them.

Again, the fragmentation of the Bible in the teaching of it is frequently such that no conception is conveyed of an on-going purpose of God in history that binds all the parts of Scripture together and reaches out beyond them to give meaning to the human story. The drama of God's dialogue with man, as it unfolds first in Israel and then in Jesus Christ moves out from Israel to all humanity, is lost to them. The Bible with its events and personages is left hanging in mid-air in a strange and distant past and the reader is expected to leap all the way across the centuries that lie between the Bible and his own world. The distance is so great that it is not surprising many fail to make the leap and for them the Bible comes close to disappearing in the mists of the past.

At this point the spread of interest in *Heilsgeschichte* (sacred history or salvation history) has made an important contribution, focusing as it does on the continuity of God's action in the life of his people not only in both Testaments but also in the life of the church.[65] It draws together into one unbroken chain the sequence of events from the creation, or from the time of Abraham, or from the birth of Israel (depending on one's definition of history), continuing sometimes clearly, sometimes hiddenly, in the life of Israel, reaching its decisive climax in Jesus Christ, and then moving forward through the centuries toward a final victory at the end of time. It has the virtue of setting us in the same stream of divine purpose and action with all the men and women of the Scriptures and with all who have come before us in the church. The Scriptures take us to the headwaters of the stream. In them a light shines in the darkness of history to reveal what God is doing with man in time. But the whole stream eventually reaches us on the growing edge of history and, insofar as we respond to God's call for a servant people in covenant relation with him and unconditionally at his disposal for the fulfillment of his redemptive purpose, we find ourselves at one with the servant people, Israel, the servant Jesus Christ, and the servant church. The Bible from beginning to end becomes the textbook of our life. Out of it we understand who we are in relation to God, to our fellowmen, and to the world.

The temptation of some scholars has been to claim too much for *Heilsgeschichte*. Oscar Cullmann[66] is not content to establish the continuity of a people of God in history in whom God's redemptive purpose has been unfolding but identifies the Biblical history of God's action in the life of his people with revelation itself, as though to know the history were to have God revealed. But the tracing of the *Heilsgeschichte* is only preparation, a setting of the stage, for the event of revelation. God is hidden in the history, even at the central point in the Biblical stream in the history of Jesus. Even the most accurate knowledge of the history and the most sympathetic understanding of it as a history of salvation will not bring God to light. The *Heilsgeschichte* at best sets us in the same world and in the same human history with prophets, psalmists, apostles, evangelists, and Jesus Christ himself, so that if our ears are opened by faith to the word that was their life, their God can be our God and their life, even the life of Jesus Christ himself, can be our life. But no history, not even sacred history, of itself is revelation.

It may seem contradictory now, having just demonstrated how a knowledge of history can help to bridge the gap between the Bible and the present day, to assert that from another aspect the modern development of historical investigation has widened the gap. Two hundred years ago the Bible seemed to provide a basis on which one could sketch the history of the world from its creation to its final consummation. The history fell into neatly balanced periods, creation being placed about 4000 B.C., Abraham 2000 years after creation, just halfway to the appearance of Jesus Christ,

and, to round out the scheme, the end of history was anticipated in A.D. 2000. But the astronomers, the archaeologists,
and the historians have put an end to such reckoning.
The astronomers speak of billions of billions of years that the
universe has been in existence. The archaeologists dig out
the bones and tools of prehistoric man some hundreds of
thousands of years ago and uncover civilizations in Palestine,
Mesopotamia, and Egypt before 4000 B.C., so that Abraham
becomes a comparative latecomer in time. Two hundred
years ago Israel stood in lonely isolation in the ancient Near
Eastern world. But today the history, literature, laws, and religion of its neighbors are known and Israel's life and history
are seen as closely interwoven with the life and history of the
surrounding nations. So also the early Christian church has
ceased to stand in isolation. The context of its birth in Judaism has become ever clearer as the literature and history of
the Jewish people in the centuries immediately before and
after the advent of Jesus have been investigated and more
accurately evaluated, especially with the help of the dis-
coveries at Qumran. And the context of its invasion of the
Gentile world and of its interaction with that world has
been laid bare by studies of the Hellenism of the first century
and of the influence of Hellenism on the traditions of the
New Testament. The first effect of all these developments
has been a great reversal in which the Biblical story has
ceased to provide a framework for world history and has become just one tiny segment in the great, rich tapestry of
world history, so closely interwoven with the surrounding
material that it is in danger of being lost from sight.[67]
We need to take account of the magnitude of this reversal of perspective and of the consequences that it brings in
its train. Biblical history, which seemed to comprehend
within its limits the story of the world from beginning to
end, is suddenly reduced to a single thread of very limited
length in the total fabric. The cozy little world that many
Christians have inhabited (in their imaginations) is broken

open on every side, to their utter consternation. They can no longer fence off the Biblical records protectively from all other human records but must apply to them the same methods of critical investigation that have proved their value in the general exploration of the past. But, more disturbing still, they cannot expect the historian to accept uncritically the Biblical author's interpretation of events any more than he would accept the interpretation given the events of his time by an Egyptian of the third millennium B.C. He has eyes only for human events, human personalities, human experiences, which he can reconstruct on the analogy of the history he observes in his own time. Therefore, when the Bible interprets the exodus from Egypt as the direct result of divine intervention, the historian has no reason to put this claim on any other level than the reports of divine intervention in their affairs by other nations in the past. The Biblical account of how the world came to be becomes just one cosmology in a complex of ancient cosmologies. The laws of the Old Testament are found to have many parallels in the law code of Hammurabi and in other ancient law codes. The translation of Egyptian proverbs discloses similarities with Israelite wisdom. A careful comparison of Jesus' teachings with those of the rabbis who were contemporary with him shows so many parallels that some scholars have been prepared to pronounce Jesus little more than a reform rabbi. Finally, so many points of contact were discovered between the teachings and practices of the early church and those of Hellenistic religious cults that there were scholars who regarded the earliest Gentile Christianity as little more than a superficially Christianized version of Hellenistic religion. The Bible, released from its isolation by modern research and set in its full historical context, has again and again seemed in danger of fading into its background and losing the uniqueness that alone justifies the claims that both Judaism and Christianity have made for it.

But the distinctiveness of the Bible can no more be lost

than Israel can die or the Christian church be extinguished. A century ago when the Babylonian stories of creation and the flood were first deciphered and their points of similarity to the accounts in Genesis observed, there was consternation in many quarters that the Bible should seem to repeat in part a Babylonian myth. But soon the comparison served to show that the distinctiveness of the Biblical accounts lay not in the detailed description of the events of creation and flood but in the theological interpretation of the world and of human existence in which the stories are clothed. The larger historical setting for Genesis, far from swallowing it up, actually released its unique witness. So also the comparison of Jesus' teachings with the teachings of the rabbis, which at first may have seemed to make him blend and begin to disappear into his Jewish background, has eventually had a double effect. It has opened our eyes more widely to the Jewishness of Jesus as a man of his own time and place in history. At the same time it makes us see that what is unique in him and in his mission is not a new religion or a new ethic but the reality of God with man creating a new humanity in the midst of history.

The natural reaction of Christians has always been a protective one when the Bible is forced out of the safety of its special religious harbor and set adrift on the sea of universal history. They fear for it, and their protectiveness may issue in a much too timid and restrained application of their historical methodology. But such fear and timidity are much more dangerous to the Scriptures and to the Christian faith than the most ruthlessly critical historical research. They betray a lack of confidence in the ability of the truth to which the Bible witnesses to maintain itself. The word of God has never needed man's defense, only the integrity of ✕ his devotion.

✕ *If God is a God of truth, why fear the truth-seekers? — that's the point, I think*

X

The Problem
of Demythologizing

Since 1941, when Rudolf Bultmann published his essay "New Testament and Mythology,"[68] the problem of demythologizing has commanded more attention than any other element in the hermeneutical discussion. There is now a very large literature on it in many languages.[69] The concentration upon it has tended to obscure the breadth of the total hermeneutical development, but it has indicated how generally and how acutely the mythological language of the New Testament is felt to constitute a serious obstacle to the preaching of the gospel.

The problem is actually just one aspect of the gap between the interpretative context of the first century and the interpretative context of today. First-century man with his three-story universe was intensely conscious of how his little world was bounded above and below by unseen worlds, above by a world of light inhabited by God and all his angels and below by a world of darkness from which emerged all manner of destructive forces to torment him. Twentieth-century man, who finds it difficult to conceive a boundary to either space or time or the existence of any realm beyond the one his science has explored, transfers the heaven and hell of ancient man from an outer world to the inner world of his experience. The devil and his demons are replaced by psychological and social factors that interfere with the functioning of the self. And at the opposite pole the logical develop-

the new dualism

ment would be for God and all the heavenly powers to be understood as symbols of constructive and creative forces in society and in the personality of man. But there is a hidden assumption of twentieth-century man at work here that controls the outcome of the translation. Reality is reduced to two dimensions: the material world without, which is the realm of the natural sciences and which man progressively masters by his science, and the experiential world within, conscious and unconscious, which the psychologists and psychiatrists explore and seek to bring under control. Banned from the outer world, God retreats into the inner world to become eventually no more than a transcendent element in man. History is the all-comprehensive reality and God is just one of the elements in history.

But there is no obligation for twentieth-century man to capitulate to this definition of reality. True, the forces that drive him in this direction are overwhelming since they already dominate the thinking of so many persons whom he respects. But, when he stands together with an Amos or an Isaiah or a Paul, he becomes aware of a dimension in reality that discloses heights and depths in his existence that are being lost from sight in the sophistication of modern scientific thought. All man's knowledge of the world without and the world within counts for nothing and leaves him empty and confused until there is added to it another knowledge, an understanding of oneself, one's fellowman and world, that is the product of a confrontation with God. Both humility and hope are born in that confrontation, and the world without as well as the world within has its character transformed. The primary reality, then, is an invisible, intangible reality, the mystery of God, which encompasses us and our world and gives meaning and purpose to our life. Far from being just an element in history, that is, in man, God is the maker of history and the maker of man. Alienated from him man loses his humanity. From this standpoint how shall we translate the three-story universe of Jesus and

Paul? No longer by dissolving heaven and hell, God and the demons, into elements merely in the inner world of man, but by recognizing the promise and the peril of our human life to be both alike constituted by our location between a world that in its absence from God and alienation from God is at the mercy of destructive and inhuman forces and a world that in the presence and by the power of God moves toward the fulfillment of a truly human life.[70] These are not figments of our imagination but are the realities between which we live our daily life, the realities that are the dynamic of our history. It is evident then that, while some form of demythologizing is a necessity in the interpretation of the Scriptures, the outcome of the process can be very different according to the nature of the assumptions that are made.

Demythologizing is made necessary also by the fact that consistently in the Biblical traditions—not in all, fortunately, but in many of them—events which take place in the personal relation between God and man are reported as though they were events in the visible external world. Paul in II Cor., ch. 12, speaks of ecstatic visions and auditions which he experienced in his relationship with Christ and we need have no hesitation in interpreting his confrontation with Christ at the time of his conversion, as reported in Acts, chs. 9; 22; and 26, as a vision. This in no way compromises the reality of the confrontation. But it does necessitate that the event should be understood as accessible to Paul alone. We can observe, however, in the reports in The Acts the marks of a process of externalization that took place as the report of the event was passed down in tradition. One account has it that the people with Paul heard a voice but saw nothing, another that they saw a light but heard nothing. The event is clearly on the way from being an event in the hidden relation between Christ and Paul to being an event in the external world where it could have been observed by anyone who was present. That it is partially hidden and partially visible lets us see the transition taking place. Similarly in Acts, ch. 2, the descent of the Spirit at Pentecost is described in terms which, while they are guarded in only *likening* the Spirit to wind and fire, have inspired pictures of the disciples with little flames sprouting from the tops of their heads. In Ex., ch. 3, which belongs plainly in sequence with Isa., ch. 6, or Jer., ch. 1, as the account of a prophetic call, the fire that superimposes itself upon a bush but does not consume it is the fiery presence of God himself, as becomes evident as God's voice sounds from the midst of the fire (even as in Paul's conversion the voice of Christ sounds from the midst of the fiery light), yet as the event is described, an externalization has taken place as though a companion of Moses might have observed the fire with equal clarity. Similarly, in the tradition of the exodus the consciousness of God's guiding presence has come to be expressed in the tradition in the visible form of the pillar of cloud by day and the pillar of fire by night.

This externalization takes place in spite of the insistence of the Scriptures that God is Spirit and cannot be seen. The result through the centuries has been a confusion concerning the nature of God's speaking and acting, a confusion that continues to the present day. But the problem has become acute in the twentieth century in a world where both nature and history are understood in a way that leaves no room for the direct intervention of God in any external fashion. The order of nature is not interrupted by heavenly invasions. Every event in history is explained from its context in a web of natural and human forces. The world of the modern scientist and historian seems to have no room for divine acts in human history. Must we, then, abandon not just this language but this whole Biblical way of understanding God's relation to the world? Langdon Gilkey[71] posed this problem sharply in an article in the *Journal of Religion* in 1961, questioning the validity of a rather widespread practice of speaking of "God's mighty acts in history" as the locus of revelation. Gordon Kaufman,[72] in answering Gilkey in 1968 in the *Harvard Theological Review,* recognizes the seriousness and inescapability of the problem for any intelligently modern man, but at the same time he sees that to abandon all belief in God's action is to abandon the living God of the Scriptures. One then goes over to an understanding of life in humanistic and naturalistic terms or to a concept of God as Being rather than Agent. Therefore he proposes to understand God's action as comprehending the whole of history, creating a context that gives profoundly different meaning to each part of it. But neither Gilkey nor Kaufman seems to see that the problem is created by the practice in Scripture of reporting events that have their reality in the personal relation between God and man in terms that depict them as though they were visible, external events. This fact has been grasped more clearly by Bultmann than by anyone else.

Gilkey couples the Biblical language concerning God's speaking together with the representations of his actions and seems convinced that we must regard both as merely religious interpretations of human events and insights. But one cannot dispose so easily of the reality of the personal relation between God and the prophet which gave birth to such language as "The word of the Lord came to me," "Hear this word the Lord has spoken," or "The Lord God showed me." The prophet represents his message as communicated to him directly by God. A conversation of Jeremiah with God is reported by the prophet himself. And certainly prophets in a state of ecstasy heard words and saw visions that were to them the very voice of God. That the content of such visions and auditions was in some measure determined by the prophetic tradition in which they stood does not detract from their validity. The prophet's eyes and ears were sharpened to see and hear by his familiarity with prophets who preceded him. We observe, however, that when the prophet's own words are before us, God's speaking takes place in the personal relation between God and the prophet and is known to others only as the prophet reports what he has heard, but when God's communication with a prophet or with any man is reported in a traditional narrative, it usually has the appearance of an audible conversation. The prophetic experience has been externalized to make of God's speech an ordinary or extraordinary historical occurrence.

A failure to take account of what has happened in these instances to the character of God's speaking and acting is fatal for the understanding of Scripture. And yet it must be granted that a large percentage of Bible readers do not even recognize what has happened. They read the text naïvely and assume that, according to the Scriptures, in Biblical times God's actions were visible and his words were audible. The Bible therefore either becomes an incredible narrative for them or it is removed to a great distance from their lives by the seeming difference between God's conduct then and now. What must be recognized is that it is the Biblical text itself that misleads them. And it is the Biblical text itself that can set them right, above all the prophets and Paul who know full well that only the eyes of faith see God's action and only the ears of faith hear his word.

Our first stage in interpretation, then, is to recognize that when the prophet speaks of seeing and hearing, it is an apprehending not with the fleshly eye or ear but with the eye and ear of the spirit. The testimony of the Fourth Gospel, "We saw his glory," is not meant to make the divine presence in Jesus visible, though Archbishop Bernard in the International Critical Commentary on John's Gospel may so understand it.[73] I John 1:1-2 insists that "we have heard, . . . we have seen with our eyes, . . . we have looked upon and touched with our hands . . . the word of life . . . the eternal life which was with the Father and was made manifest to us," but we are not misled by the language into making eternal life tangible! This is the language of faith in which men bear witness to a reality more immediate and meaningful to them than the objects that surround them.

And when the text of Scripture gives God a visible form as a majestic king, or as a pillar of fire, or as a dove descending from above, we readily transfer the images back again from the external world to the world of personal relation. This is a form of demythologizing, but the question is still open whether we interpret the visions and auditions as merely projections of man's thoughts and insights into a realm beyond himself or as the disclosure to him of a presence that not only forms the hidden boundary of our world but is the source from which alone our world finds its completion. Again what decides the final issue of the demythologizing is the conception of reality held by the interpreter. If for him there is no reality beyond the world of nature and history, then the voice to which the prophet and the apostle hearken with such awe and utter devotion is just the inner voice of their own higher natures, their reason or their conscience, which one may or may not grace with the name of God. But if this be incredible to us, if for us as for all the Biblical witnesses the ultimate and disastrous illusion of man is the identification of anything in himself with God, if we know at the base of our own life a relationship with God in which the only life worth having has to be given to us from beyond ourselves, we do not find ourselves so far removed from the prophet and apostle. We may not have visions or auditions (though they may occur), but we too live in utter dependence upon the word which we cannot speak to ourselves but have to have spoken to us. It is mediated to us by human words and yet it is the word of God. And we ourselves may speak words to others which become for them a mediating of God's own word. For the preacher it is of great importance in his understanding of his ministry which conception of reality determines the outcome of his interpretation.

These examples are sufficient to make plain both the necessity of demythologizing in the interpretation of Scripture and the importance of the interpreter's theology in determining the outcome of the process. The failure to demythologize is the failure to interpret and it leaves a large part of Scripture entangled and obscured in a conceptuality that is meaningless to the man of today. Frequently as one listens to a passage of Scripture being read in church, one has the impression of someone speaking in a foreign tongue in some strange and distant world. The words cry out for interpretation, but so often no interpretation is forthcoming and the congregation goes away even more convinced than before of its inability to make sense of Scripture. As such experiences are repeated, a massive block builds up in the mind and serves to keep the Scriptures closed. Bultmann is right that the language of Scripture becomes a needless rock of offense barring the access of man to the gospel and alienating him from the Scriptures, so that he no longer is exposed to the truly offensive word that has in it both God's judgment upon his past and his promise for the future.

But demythologizing as taught by Bultmann takes on a special character as a consequence of the theological context in which it is practiced. It is significant that for him, as for some of his disciples such as Herbert Braun and James M. Robinson, demythologizing and existential interpretation are inseparable.[74] The two are spoken of as though they were a single process. Existential interpretation, however, is the consequence of a philosophical and theological decision that so affirms the hiddenness of God that no tenable statement can be made by man concerning God. All such statements are categorized as mythological. Knowledge of God is then impossible for man. All he can know is what happens in his experience and in his understanding of his own existence when he is exposed to God's action in the gospel. Demythologizing now becomes a highly complex operation. The mythological statements are not to be dismissed (as they were by nineteenth-century liberalism) but are to be interpreted, for they contain the witness, in the only language first-century man could command, to the decisive action of God. There has to be extracted from them the understanding of existence which they express, which then can be translated into terms that are comprehensible to men who live in a world that has left behind the mythologies of an earlier age.

Bultmann himself struggles hard to maintain the reality of a "Beyond" and of a word from the Beyond in which alone human life has hope of its fulfillment, in spite of his assertion of their total hiddenness from man. But in the work of Herbert Braun, which meets with Bultmann's approval, the "Beyond" which transcends the world is on its way to becoming only the transcendent element in the human person and one sees on the horizon a recrudescence of the immanentalism of the nineteenth and early twentieth centuries which Bultmann, like Barth, was anxious and determined to overcome. The radical negation of traditional doctrines by Bultmann and his disciples, which has so frightened many churchmen in Germany and has generated a strongly reactionary conservative movement, is the consequence not of the necessities of demythologizing but of the theological assumptions implicit in an existentialist philosophy.

This is particularly evident in Bultmann's interpretation of Biblical statements concerning God as creator.[75] Insofar as God's creative activity is described in anthropomorphic terms as though he appeared in person and at certain times brought specific objects into being, we can readily agree to the need for demythologizing. But such naïveté is not characteristic of the Biblical faith in God as creator. The psalmist describes the shaping of the child in the womb as God's creative act. The prophet describes the birth of Israel as a servant-people of God, the destruction that overtook the nation and the future vindication of God's purpose for his people as all of them creative acts of God. Both Gen., ch. 1, and John, ch. 1, in representing God as creating through his word, have already demythologized the primitive concept and are expressing a profound theological understanding of the relation between God and the world. What Bultmann rejects as mythological, however, is *any* statement that relates God to the world as creator to creation. Since God is wholly hidden from man except insofar as in the hearing of the gospel man experiences in himself a change in his self-understanding, all such statements are inadmissible. Therefore, in calling God the creator, the most a Christian can mean is that God is *his* creator in freeing him from his past and opening to him a new future. The same objection would apply to the frequent Old Testament statements concerning God's action in history. Israel's consciousness of its destiny rested on the conviction that in the events of the exodus God had acted in love to redeem his people from slavery, and the narrative of the subsequent history consists largely of a succession of such acts. Undoubtedly Bultmann's strange judgment that the Old Testament was divine revelation for Israel but cannot be considered revelation by Christians was the consequence of his rejection as mythology of all such statements in the Old Testament concerning God as creator and Lord of history. It must be granted that the Old Testament is a shambles when that one element is eliminated.

But why was it eliminated? The reason is quite apparent in Bultmann's theology: first, in his negation of all statements concerning God's relation to the world and to events in history, and secondly, in his insistence that God touches man's life only on its inner side where the decisions are made and not in the outer events that happen to him. So far as the external world and its history are concerned, Bultmann seems to abandon it as a subject for theological consideration. It is significant that in his eschatology the Biblical goal of history becomes merely the goal toward which the individual Christian moves as successive confrontations with the gospel emancipate him from his inauthentic past; mankind seems no longer to have any goal, or at least the Christian is restrained from making any statements about it. The loss to Christian faith is immense. Certainly the idea has to be abandoned that God as creator and ruler of the universe controls events from behind the scenes so that everything that happens is to be attributed to his direct action. The cross should be sufficient to put an end to that idea. But the faith that overcomes the world in both Old Testament and New is a faith that God meets us and deals with us not just in the events of the inner world of self but also in the events of the outer world of time and history. The inner and outer worlds are inseparable.

The unfortunate result, then, of the fusing of the project of demythologizing with existential interpretation by Bultmann and his followers is a disastrous confusing of the minds of men as to what is actually involved in demythologizing. It is an urgent task that has been too long neglected. But if men are persuaded that they cannot demythologize without committing themselves to the theological principles of an existential interpretation, the task is likely to continue to be neglected, deliberately neglected, in most areas of the church.

XI

No Scripture,
No Revelation!

T HE PROBLEM that we set out to investigate *so far* was the growing silence of the Scriptures in the life of the church and in the consciousness of Christian people. The argument, very briefly, has been (a) that the general growth of *the modern mind* knowledge and of man's understanding of himself and his history which has taken place during the past two hundred years has created such a gap between the language and concepts of the Bible and the language and concepts of modern man that, unassisted, he cannot make adequate sense of what he reads; (b) that during these two hundred years *scholar/* Biblical scholars have faced with courage the complex prob- *man in* lems that the text of Scripture furnishes for the modern *the pew* mind and have amassed a wealth of knowledge that en- *hiatus* ables one to read any part of it intelligently, but, for various reasons, this knowledge has not in general been permitted to reach the membership of the church, so that to a large extent the Bible for them no longer belongs in the age in which they actually live; (c) that Biblical scholarship itself con- *the short-* tributed to this process of alienation unintentionally in that, *coming of* in its endeavor to be scientifically objective in its analysis of *biblical* the literature and its reconstruction of the history and re- *scholarship* ligion, it neglected the theological content of the text which alone secures its relevance for succeeding ages; (d) that advances have been made in Biblical interpretation in the past fifty years to take more adequate account of both the histori-

another problem with biblical scholarship

cal and the theological content of the text, but this promising development has been hindered, particularly in America, by the suspicion among Biblical scholars that it undermines the scientific character of Biblical scholarship, so that again the tools of a more adequate interpretation are withheld from the church; (e) that what is most urgently needed is a reopening of the hermeneutical question by scholars, with the most thorough discussion of its every aspect, and the mediating of a more adequate hermeneutic to the membership of the church. All in all, the goal is for preacher and people together to face honestly what is there before them in the Scriptures, an openness to the problems of the literature and history bringing in its train an openness to the revolutionary word that awaits them in the text.

what is needed

The objection may be made, however, that the effect of our hermeneutical discussion is to extend the alienation of the modern mind from the text of Scripture rather than to overcome it.[76] We have insisted so constantly on the distinction between the Scriptures themselves and the revelation of God's presence and action in human life to which they witness that we may have created the impression that the revelation is somehow behind and beyond the words of Scripture rather than that it comes to us in the words. The reality of revelation is "God with man in the midst of his history" and it is obvious that that reality by its nature cannot be transferred to writings in a book, any such transference being in some measure an abstraction. That the revelation can be mediated through the writings in a book to another age in history is another matter. But the distinction between the writings and the revelation is essential and must be preserved. The revelation is primarily an illumination of the relationship of man with God and with his fellowman. It is the truth of that relationship, but it is also the life that is the gift of God to man in that relationship. Before there was an Old Testament there was an Israel that had found the secret of living and not dying in an unconditional open-

ness to God, yet in century after century was torn between
faithfulness and rebellion, in both responses bearing witness
to the reality of the covenant relation. And before there could
be a New Testament there had to be a presence of God with
man in Jesus Christ that generated in his disciples the conviction and the consciousness of a new day dawning in the
relationships between God and man and between man and
man on which the whole structure of human existence rests.
But we create a serious illusion if we leave in men's minds the
impression that there is any other way, any direct and un-
mediated way, for us to find access to this reality of revelation
in history except through the reading and the exposition
of the text of Scripture itself.

Again, in emphasizing that the revelation is *hidden* in the
history so that even the most authentic reconstruction of the
history of Israel or of the history of Jesus and his church
fails to penetrate the depths in which it is hidden, we may
seem to be pointing to an obscure region *behind* the history
that lies *behind* the text that we hold in our hands. Many
who readily accept the first distinction between the revelation
and the book find this second one between the revelation
and the history frustrating and mystifying. They remain convinced that if a revelation of God was given to Israel, then
it should be identifiable with elements that are discernible
in the reconstructed history of Israel—insights, values, ideas,
and beliefs—and that if Jesus in his person and teachings
constitutes the ultimate in revelation, it should be possible
to validate the claim by setting forth his history. The long
succession of lives of Jesus illustrates both the zeal with which
men have tried to make visible the revelation in which the
Christian faith and church have had their origin and the
success with which that revelation has maintained its resistance to such attempts. Already in the New Testament
traditions, and even more vividly in the apocryphal writings
of the first century, we see the conviction at work that the
divine presence and power must have been visible in Jesus'

person and action. But contradicting that whole way of thinking is the consistent witness at the heart of the New Testament traditions that the mystery of God's presence in Jesus Christ was revealed only to faith and was long concealed even from those who seemed to be closest to him. Are we left then with a revelation that is somehow concealed in the history that is to be excavated from behind the text?

If this is where our hermeneutic leaves us, then we have accentuated the problem instead of moving toward its solution. What must be kept in sight at every stage of our dealings with Scripture is that the revelation of God and man that was reality in Israel and that in Jesus Christ burst its national limitations to become the faith and life of all mankind has access to each new age only through the narrow channel of Scripture. It is not to be equated with a book, but it comes to us only through the medium of that book and, when the book is no longer read and understood by Christians, they have been cut off decisively from the roots of their distinctively Christian existence. Therefore we need, perhaps, to retrace our steps somewhat and establish more clearly the relation of the revelation to the text of Scripture that makes a knowledge of the Scriptures necessary and indispensable to the Christian.

There has in the past been an extended argument between theologians concerning which came first, the Scriptures or the church. The one side contended that, since the church was there before there were any Scriptures and the Scriptures were written by the church, the church is primary, and the other that, since the gospel which is remembered in the Scriptures was there before there was a church and called the church into being, the Scriptures which witness to the gospel are primary. The one has traditionally depreciated the importance of the Scriptures and contributed to their neglect; the other has depreciated the importance of the church and trusted the Scriptures and preaching to do what only a living church can do. However, both the Scriptures and the church alike are essential to the revelation.

By God's call to Israel and Israel's response the covenant relationship was established that was the foundation of Israel's life. But the relationship was sustained through traditions in which not only the call and the faithfulness of God in his relation with Israel but also the alternating faithfulness and unfaithfulness of Israel were remembered and in solemn ceremonies were rehearsed in the hearing of the people. The call was repeated again and again by prophets, each repetition being a call to repentance that the relation with God, broken by rebellion, might be restored, and the prophet's words in turn were taken up into the tradition. The traditions were constantly reinterpreted in the context of the growing clarity of Israel's faith. The prophets stood in the full stream of the tradition but they were not imprisoned in it. Priests were more likely to be imprisoned, but the immediacy of the prophet's relation with God preserved his freedom to speak a new word to the new situation. Again, there were the responses of Israelites to God in prayer and praise that became the formal responses of the nation in its worship and a powerful continuing witness to the covenant relation. The tradition was alive and growing as the expression of Israel's faith and at the same time it became the authoritative definition of that faith as witness to the nature of God's relation not just with Israel but with all men. But always both the tradition and the covenant relation to which it witnessed were open-ended and forward-looking. The destiny inherent in Israel's call created visions of a future yet to be revealed and a work of God yet to be accomplished. Israel like Abraham was a venturer into an unknown future. The dynamic of the relation with God would not let Israel rest but drove it ever forward. Essential to this movement of Israel as the people of God in history is the remembering of its past relationship with God. Israel looked backward in order to move forward. The vision of the future was born in the remembrance of the past. Therefore we must say that without the tradition that is now embodied in the Old Testament there could have been no Israel. The sacred Scriptures were necessary to its life.

On the threshold of the New Testament we receive a warning of the peril to the revelation when the dialectic between the witness of the tradition and the continuing reality of revelation in the community of faith is dissolved. The movement forward is stopped. The faith of the community becomes frozen in its structures. The tradition is equated with the revelation so that there is no longer room in it for a John the Baptist or a Jesus. The God of the covenant relation is worshiped at a distance and is no longer expected to be present and active in the midst of his people. Against this background we see how Jesus restored the dialectic of revelation. He liberated God from his imprisonment in the tradition. He left behind no writings of his own, for he himself had bitter experience of how Scriptures could become a tyrant and a barrier against the living presence and power of God. But, in asking his disciples at the Last Supper to remember him, he anticipated a new tradition and was aware of its necessity.

What happened in Jesus Christ, in his relation with persons, in his impact on his disciples, in his controversy with opponents, in the drama of his death and resurrection, and in his continuing mission in and through his church, is more like an explosion than what we usually think of as a revelation. It is like an invasion from another world that turns things topsy-turvy. It stuns men, frightens them, inverts their values, makes traitors out of good men and heroes out of cowards. And all because Jesus announces the presence of God with man in the midst of man's history! The heart of Jesus' gospel was a reinterpretation of the reality that had been the heart of Israel's existence from the beginning—God with man and man with God—but what made it new was that in his person the contradiction between man and God that had been Israel's recurrent tragedy and man's agonizing dilemma was overcome and a human life was joyfully fulfilled in God. The word of God that had in it all the promise of man's future was the very substance of his life. To be confronted by him, to hear him speak, was to be made aware of the radical contradiction between oneself (and one's world) and God and at the same time to be met by a love in which God himself was reaching out to reestablish his covenant relationship with man. The revelation was reality in him and through him in the community of faith that had its origin from him.

But the explosive event of revelation did not create an orderly development. The Book of The Acts on its surface gives the impression of a development in a direct line from Jesus to a universal church, but, beneath its surface and supplemented by Paul's letters and extracanonical traditions, the evidence produces for us a picture of diverse and in many respects contradictory movements that originated with Jesus. Faithful and devoted Christians were not all agreed in their interpretation of the significance of Jesus or in their definition of the faith that had been generated in response to him. There was unity in their awareness of a new life, both with God and in their relations with their fellowmen, that had been opened to them by him, but they had yet to draw out all the implications of that new life.

The authoritative interpretation and definition was to take the remainder of the century and, as they remembered, interpreted, and defined, a new tradition came into being. There were interpretations and definitions that were attempted but eventually had to be rejected because the church did not recognize in them a valid witness to the revelation from which it had its life. And there were elements in some of the writings that were eventually included in the New Testament that made the church uncertain for a time whether these writings were necessary and essential to its definition of its faith. But what is clear from the story of the shaping of the New Testament canon is that in the New Israel, the church, the same process was repeated as in the Old Testament. The revelation, which was the continuing presence of God in the midst of his people, shaped not only a people but also a tradition as that people remembered God's presence and action in their midst in the past. The past was seen not in separation from the present but always in the light of God's presence and action in the present. As in John's Gospel, past and present merge and point toward the future. The Christian gospel, faith, and church are defined not merely by what Jesus was and did and said in his lifetime but also by what he continued to be to his people and to say in their hearts and to do in their midst. It is no accident that the *risen* Lord is central to the life of the early church, for the risen Lord is the name of the living God in his continuing presence in the community of faith. That continuing presence in history, then, is the reality of the Christian revelation, but it is sustained only as the church in its tradition, whether it be gospels, letters, or history, continues to remember the events in which it had its origin. In its tradition the church defined its faith and drew a line around the writings in which it recognized the essential witness to the revelation which would be the perennial source of its renewal and its unity. The tradition, however, was kept from becoming a prison house for faith by the consciousness that the living, life-transforming presence of the risen Lord was with his people in his church and not just in the book by means of which his people kept fresh the remembrance of him. The dialectic between the Scriptures and the community of faith had to be maintained if the revelation was to retain its dynamic as the unfolding of a divine purpose in human history.

The dialectic has still to be maintained. To insist that revelation is wholly in the Scriptures is to repeat the error of first-century Judaism and to deny the Bible's own definition of God's revealing presence. And invariably and inevitably it produces a static Christianity. Belief in the resurrection of Jesus Christ becomes merely belief in an event that happened centuries ago rather than an openness to the God who reconciled and reconciles our humanity and our world to himself in Jesus Christ. But equally the dialectic is destroyed when the Scriptures fall silent. The conviction of Christ's continuing presence in the church has sometimes been affirmed as though it were so embodied in the empirical church that it would continue quite apart from any hearing of the Scriptures. But what issues from that conviction is again a church that identifies its dogmas and its structures with the revelation and becomes imprisoned in them. Freedom for God and for the fulfillment of its destiny as the servant of God's purpose in the world is preserved within the church only when the church by means of the Scriptures is kept conscious of its Lord and hears him speaking in each new situation that confronts it. No Scriptures, no church! No Scriptures, no revelation!

It is this necessity of the Scriptures to the existence of the church and to the continuity of God's presence and action in history that comes to expression in the traditional practice of calling the Bible the word of God. But there is so much in Scripture in which men can hear no word of God, or which seems to contradict the gospel as we hear it from Jesus Christ, that many have rebelled against that practice or have regarded it as no more than a "courtesy title." The formula that has been most popular as an alternative is that the Bible *contains* the word of God. This provides each reader of the Scriptures with the convenient device of a canon within the canon within which he can place the passages that seem to him to deepen and strengthen the Christian faith while he relegates to the outer corridor everything that distresses and perplexes him. It recognizes frankly that the words from the mouth of God which are man's meat and drink are not found everywhere in Scripture but have to be searched for like gold in a mine and separated from all that is not gold. The unfortunate result, however, of the erection of a canon within the canon is that each man now has his private canon of Scripture. He recognizes as "the word of God for him" such passages of Scripture as have the most appeal to him. But what he needs most to hear is often hidden in the parts that are most distasteful to him. The word of God has in it always elements that are congenial and elements that are uncongenial since it is at one and the same time God's words of both judgment and grace, no grace without the judgment and no judgment without the grace. To eliminate the uncongenial may be to escape the judgment that makes us ready to receive the grace. This is a peril also of the preacher. Nothing so impoverishes his preaching as a constant dwelling in a narrow circle of texts that are his favorites. The canon within the canon can become a wall shutting us inside a Scripture that we have unconsciously selected to be the basis and the confirmation not only of a most limited and inadequate theology but also of an inadequate church. The Scriptures are more likely to be the word of God to us and to the church, setting us in motion ever afresh toward the fulfillment of our destiny, if we respect the limits that the church determined for the canon, marking off from all other books a selection in which across the centuries it heard most clearly the word that created, nourished, and sustained it in its journey. These are the books in which it found itself defined, not by men but in the relationship of God with men in generation after generation. Not everything in the books is word of God, but neglect of any of them may silence for us something that is essential to the hearing of the word that created both Israel and the Christian church and can make us today a church worthy of that succession.

XII

How the Bible
Becomes Contemporary

IT IS NOT SURPRISING that for many people today the Bible
belongs to a world that we have left far behind us. The
advances of modern knowledge are so great and the pace
has been so accelerated in many areas that for the younger
generation even the early twentieth century seems to belong
to a remote past. Recently some youthful theological experts
were heard declaiming that since 1964 we have passed
into a new era in which even the greatest theologians
who lived before that date have only a minor significance.
Why they chose the year 1964 was left somewhat vague,
but their consciousness of having been emancipated from a
complex and burdensome past was bright and clear. This
mood is fed from many sources. In transportation have we
not moved in one short lifetime from the horse and buggy
age to supersonic jets and rockets which make the journey
to the moon? In medicine the advances in research are
so rapid that the doctor who is ten years out of date is a peril
to his patients. In engineering, in education, in business,
the knowledge imparted by competent teachers yesterday
is no longer adequate today. And yet the church officially
—regardless of what it does in actuality—asks men to believe that the last word concerning man's relation with
God and with his fellowman is set down in writings which
were complete by the end of the first century A.D.! In the
light of what has been happening in all other realms of

human knowledge the claim must seem outrageous. And like so many other things in the Christian faith, such as belief in a Creator, or the assertion that a Jew from Nazareth represents the climax of God's purpose in history, or the expectation of a new humanity and a new world through him, it *is* outrageous—unless it is valid and true.

The preacher is up against this mood which consigns the Bible to the past. He meets it not only in his hearers but also in himself. He may have met it also in some of his Biblical and theological teachers. A leading Christian educator a few years ago was heard to say often, "We have passed so far beyond the prophets and Jesus that it is ridiculous to regard them as in any way authorities for our religion." A frequent complaint of theological students concerns the vagueness of the relation between what they learn in their Biblical studies and the theological constructions that are intended to be their equipment for Christian thinking. And, as we have already seen, it is possible for the Biblical scholar to be so engrossed in his task of historical description that the Bible for his students becomes largely a bundle of curious archaeological specimens. Or, having learned from him to decipher accurately the original meaning of texts, they may be so appalled by the frequency with which preachers and teachers secure a relevance for the Biblical text by appending to it a meaning that it does not contain that they despair of doing well what others do so badly. It is essential therefore to the preacher that he see not only that there is a content in Scripture which has demonstrated over and over its ability to become contemporary, but also *how*, in spite of the time-conditioned character of the language and concepts in which that content finds expression, it finds its freedom and relevance in a different era.

The Bible itself is a massive demonstration of how Scripture becomes contemporary, covering as it does a period of more than a thousand years during which the people on whom the story centers experienced profound changes. The one element that remained constant through those centuries was the covenant relation, the reality of a personal bond between an unseen God and a people that knew itself claimed by him for his service. Sometimes the community in which the bond was sustained was reduced to a tiny fragment of the nation but never was it extinguished. Always there was a community of some kind in which the traditions concerning God's dealings with his people in the past were preserved. But they were not preserved intact and unmodified. A distinctive feature of the traditions preserved in both Testaments is that they were constantly being reinterpreted. In fourteen centuries or more the community of faith moved through many phases and was exposed to a succession of different civilizations. It was born in the desert and found the earliest formulations of its faith in the bare life of the desert. From there it moved to Palestine where it had to withstand the pressures of a Canaanite culture technically superior to it but utterly alien to its faith. Gradually in outward organization it moved from a form of tribal confederation with a tenuous existence to become a powerful monarchy, which soon degenerated however into a pair of quarrelsome petty states, almost constantly under tribute to a powerful neighbor. Such dependency meant exposure to the culture and religious influence of a succession of dominant states: Egypt, Assyria, Babylonia, Persia, Greece, Syria, and Rome. Each left its mark upon the community, sometimes a very deep mark, but none proved capable of interrupting or destroying the continuity of the faith-tradition that lay at the core of the community's life. There was in it a resiliency and a mobility that made it able to reformulate itself in each new age in a way relevant and appropriate to the age, and often the reformulation meant a widening and deepening of the tradition. We need to examine several instances of such reformulation.

The two stories of creation in Genesis provide us with two interpretations of the same theme five hundred years apart.

the analogy to the two creation accounts in Genesis

①

The earlier account bears clearly upon it the marks of its origin among a people more familiar with deserts than with rivers and in an age that made free use of mythological concepts, trees whose fruit confers life and knowledge of good and evil, a god who walks the earth among men, a snake who tempts men to evil. These concepts are used not naïvely but with a profound theological significance to interpret to man his situation in a world where his life is continually obstructed by evil and to disclose to him the source of his dilemma in the rupture of his relation of openness and trust with his creator through his inordinate claim to independence. God is Creator; man is creature, dependent for his health and for the health of the personal relations in which he has his life upon his relation with his creator; and the world is the scene in which the drama of these relations is to be played out. To the Priestly author of five hundred years later this was not a satisfactory account of the creation. He had no quarrel with its theology but only with its conceptuality. The earlier author had lived in the narrow and primitive world of the Davidic or Solomonic kingdom. The later author belongs to a nation that is scattered across the world and he comprehends the whole wide world in his range of vision. His God no longer walks the earth or shapes clay to make a man. From his heavenly dwelling place in the unseen he has only to speak his word and what he wills is accomplished. God is Creator as before but now the focus of his creative action is not just upon the first ancestors of mankind but upon the totality of things, and God's provision for order in his world is through a humanity that in its personal relation with its Creator will reflect on earth the qualities of his nature.

There is no basic quarrel theologically between the two accounts. Though separated by so many centuries, they belong together in the continuity of the same tradition of faith and understanding. The one speaks in the language and thought forms and to the concerns of one age, the other in the language and thought forms and to the concerns of a very different age, and between the two of them they point us in the direction in which we have to go if, in our own age, vastly different from both of them, we would bring the same essential realities to expression. The world with its origin and destiny hidden in the purpose of God; God's creative power which is able to transform a chaos into an ordered world; man the creature of God, wholly dependent upon him so that obedience is the secret of his life and yet created for a relationship with God so intimate that he should speak God's word after him and reign on God's behalf in the creation; these realities have to be liberated in age after age from the concepts of an earlier age and reexpressed in language in which men can recognize themselves, their world, and the God whose creative action is not bound to the concepts of any one age.

The Scriptures mark out for us the continuity of the tradition. We do not have just these first three chapters of Genesis for our guidance. The same faith comes to expression again and again. It meets us in a very succinct form in the Eighth Psalm. Second Isaiah builds on it constantly as he encourages his despondent people to expect a new creative action of God that will set not just a scattered Israel but the whole of humanity on its way toward its redemption. The author of the Fourth Gospel reinterprets the creation in the light of what had been revealed concerning God's creative and transforming power in the Incarnate Word, in Jesus Christ. A whole succession of witnesses speak to us of what it meant to them to know God as the Creator and themselves as his creatures. We have to give them their freedom to speak, each in the language of his own age and his own immediate situation, and, when we do, we find that it is no impediment to our sharing of their faith. But, when we have shared their faith, they confer on us not just the freedom but also the responsibility of expressing that faith in the language of our own age. It is sad that so many Christians are still imprisoned by the idea that to share the Biblical faith in the Creator they have to share in some degree the primitive conceptualities of twenty-five hundred years ago when, as a matter of fact, it is intrinsic to the nature of the Biblical faith at every point that it sits loosely to all time-conditioned conceptualities.

Equally illuminating is what is made of the figure of Abraham in both Testaments. Undoubtedly there was a historical ancestor of Israelites, and of more than Israelites, named Abraham, who migrated from the Mesopotamian region westward, but as he appears in the traditions of Israel he has become the incarnation of the destiny of Israel, a figure in whose story Israel for centuries saw as in a mirror its own relationship with God. Abraham's call to become the agent of God's redemptive purpose in the world was one with Israel's call. Abraham's temptations were Israel's temptations, and God's promises to Abraham were God's promises to Israel. It is no longer possible in the records to distinguish between the faith of Abraham and the faith of Israel as it remembered Abraham. The formula in Deut. 26:5-10 which was recited at each harvest festival identified Abraham with the whole succession that stemmed from him. Abraham became the nation in bondage in Egypt and, as the later confessor recited the story of his nation's deliverance, he did not say "God delivered them" but "God delivered us," seeing himself and the people of his later time as participating in the earlier decisive events in continuity with Abraham. The consciousness of continuity and identity with Abraham in faith and destiny was the basis on which the Abraham stories were able to make themselves contemporary with ever-new generations. The Jewish contemporaries of John the Baptist and Jesus made of this continuity with Abraham ("We are children of Abraham") an endorsement of their religious establishment, exempting them from any need to respond to a fresh call of God. They identified with Abraham formally but not with the faith of which he was a representation and witness and of which both John the Baptist and Jesus were contemporary expressions. To stand truly in the faith-tradition of Abraham

The analogy to Isaiah 53

2)

was in the first century A.D. to be willing like Abraham to break with the past at the call of God and to launch out at his command into an unknown future. Therefore both Paul and the author of Hebrews seized upon Abraham as a symbol of the new Israel of God, the church. In Abraham's story they saw the expression of a faith in which man is bound so unconditionally to God's purpose for the world that he can never become complacent about his own spiritual attainments, can never be content with any established order, but, drawn on by the vision of the city of God, is committed to an ever-renewed pilgrimage toward the goal. The Abraham of Paul and of Hebrews is the eternal contemporary.

A third instance of how Scripture becomes contemporary is the fifty-third chapter of Isaiah and what happened to it as the Christian church tried to understand the ministry, death, and resurrection of Jesus. There is no need to insist that, in spite of its origin being nearly six centuries removed from the time of Jesus, it became vividly contemporary for Jesus and the early church, so contemporary that it has always been hard for Christians to realize that it was written for any other occasion. We have to make a strenuous effort to restore the chapter to its original context in the ministry and writings of a prophet of the sixth century B.C. There it is the climax of Second Isaiah's interpretation of what it means to be a people of God, the servant of God's word, in the midst of a hostile and alienated world. The word in which is hidden not just God's gracious purpose for his world but also the power to bring that purpose to fulfillment, has been entrusted to poor, broken little Israel. It is unbelievable, yet true. And what deepens the mystery still further is that to serve God's word with faithfulness is to be set in such contradiction to the mass of mankind that one is scorned, trampled upon, and perhaps even sent to one's death. Yet only through such unconditional faithfulness in his servant can God open the blind eyes of men and overcome their alienation from him. It is at once obvious why that chapter became overwhelmingly contemporary in the early church. The servant of the word envisaged by Second Isaiah was actual in Jesus. Jesus was in almost every detail what the prophet described. But we cannot stop there. Our question is how that chapter becomes contemporary now. If we apply it exclusively to Jesus, we have lost a large part of both its original and its Christian meaning. It is significant that in the New Testament, when Jesus uses the Servant image, or others use it in regard to him, he and his disciples are included together in the scope of it.[77] He is the Servant that they in union with him may be servants. The servant of the word is the people of God in every age. Jesus Christ is the climactic fulfillment of the destiny of this people of God. In both Israel and the church the identification of the community of faith with the Servant is always broken and ambiguous, having to be healed by repentance and forgiveness. Faithfulness is always compromised by unfaithfulness. But in Jesus himself all ambiguity and brokenness are gone. God and his Servant are at one. Therefore we read Isa., ch. 53, in the light of its New Testament fulfillment, but it does not begin to be contemporary for us until it spells out not just the destiny of Jesus but also our destiny as his church in the midst of a hostile and alienated world which he means to redeem.

The entire ministry and teaching of Jesus can be understood as an example of the Scriptures becoming contemporary. This is partially concealed by the infrequency of Jesus' quotations from Scripture. Men remarked on the fact that, whereas the rabbis were constantly quoting Scripture to give authority to their statements, Jesus spoke directly as though an authority resided in his own words that was in no way inferior to the authority of Moses or the prophets. But what Jesus said and did was a living reinterpretation and reformulation of the essential content of the Old Testament. To detach the word of God heard in Jesus' ministry from the word of God in the Scriptures of the Old Testament does violence to every strand of tradition in the New Testament.

There is no Jesus Christ anywhere in the New Testament who is not the fulfillment of everything that is promised and hoped for in the Old Testament. He gathers up in himself and his gospel and brings to its culmination the word which every Old Testament voice is straining to speak. Their words are not yet his word and yet it is his word that haunts their words and continually seeks to break through. Jesus' rare quotation of the Old Testament dare not be misunderstood. It must be seen in the full prophetic and apostolic context. The prophets did not quote their predecessors but spoke directly what they heard from God as they stood in continuity with their predecessors. Paul did not quote Jesus, yet who can fail to see that Paul was saturated with the gospel of Jesus which came to its most forceful expression in his death and resurrection? In the hands of the rabbis the Scriptures had been in danger of becoming a revered religious relic from the past which froze the community of faith into one permanently unchangeable form. What Jesus did was to break them open and let the word of God come forth from them with a freshness and power that created nothing less than a new beginning in the life of humanity.

Jesus' ministry was within the context of Judaism. He looked beyond the confines of his own nation to the whole world, just as Second Isaiah had done, but in his lifetime he restricted his mission and that of his disciples to his Jewish people. Its focus was on the outsiders among them who for various reasons were excluded from the religious community. There were a few rare occasions when a Gentile responded to him, calling forth from him an exclamation of delight, but he remained a worshiper in synagogue and temple with his mission concentrated on the reclaiming of Israel as the Servant of God's redemptive purpose in the world. As a consequence a conservative section of the earliest Jerusalem church considered its gospel to be inseparable from the essentially Jewish formulation in which it was first expressed. But within the first generation, in fact within only a few years of the death of Jesus, the mission was carried beyond the bounds of Judaism into the Gentile world which was Greek not only in its language but in all its ways of thinking. The ability of the gospel to make itself comprehensible in a totally new interpretative context was challenged in the most radical way. But the New Testament text presents to us the results of the reinterpretation. So largely is it the reinterpretation for the Gentile world that we have to delve beneath the surface to discover the character of the earliest mission and preaching as it existed in a purely Jewish context.

The letters of Paul and the Gospel of John provide us with two vivid examples of reinterpretation. Christians who think the Gospel should be fixed in one unchangeable form if it is to sustain its integrity are likely to be badly shaken if they open their eyes to what Paul and the author of the Fourth Gospel actually did. So different is Paul's formulation of the gospel from that of Jesus and so rarely does he refer to anything that Jesus said or did that some scholars have set in question his continuity with Jesus. William Wrede[78] held that Paul knew nothing of Jesus except the fact of his death and did not want to know anything of him that he might with complete freedom formulate a gospel for the Gentile world. But this is nonsense. It was Paul's awareness of the revolutionary character of the mission of Jesus that made him become, first, in loyalty to the religious establishment, the persecutor of Christians, and then, on his conversion, the apostle of that revolutionary mission to the Gentile world. Never for a moment did he let his continuity with Jesus be set in doubt nor did he let that continuity take from him his freedom to give fresh formulation to the gospel in the new context. The author of the Fourth Gospel exercised the same freedom and maintained the same continuity. From beginning to end his presentation of Jesus in his ministry and teaching, death and resurrection, is distinctively his own, a profound reinterpretation of Jesus for a somewhat

Hellenized Jewish Christian community. When one compares its details with the Synoptic Gospels the differences are so many that they defy all attempts at harmonization. And yet it is not a different person who meets us in the Fourth Gospel, but the same person mediated to us through the witness of a church that had a very different context and tradition.

What amazes us about both Paul and the author of the Fourth Gospel is that, in formulating the gospel in their new situations with such freedom, they were able to preserve their continuity with Jesus and with the original mission with such integrity and power. The peril of every reinterpretation is illustrated for us by Marcion in the middle of the second century. In his endeavor to make the gospel meaningful in a Greek world, he claimed the freedom of a Paul and a John, but his continuity was not, like theirs, a continuity with a Jesus whose mission was the fulfillment of the word that for over a thousand years had been lodged in Israel's heart, but rather a continuity with a Greek theology of which he made Jesus the bearer. His hostility to the Old Testament is an indication of how intolerable that basic Biblical continuity was to him. There is a warning for us in this, that a reinterpretation that is attempted without first finding the continuity of our own community of faith with *both* Israel and the New Testament church is in danger of producing a gospel that is only too easily assimilable to the dominant ideology of the cultural context.

The history of the church provides any number of illustrations of the Bible becoming contemporary. The most dramatic one, of course, is the Protestant Reformation. The text of the Scriptures had become buried in medieval times under a mass of authoritative interpretations until it was impossible for even such an earnest and searching mind as that of Luther to get at its essential message. The Bible had become little more than a sounding board echoing the mind of the religious establishment and providing it with unchallengeable divine authority. It validated the massive and overwhelmingly impressive order of life established by the church. Luther at first in his lectures on the Bible interpreted it in that context. But as he began to go behind the Latin translation to the original Greek and Hebrew; and behind the accepted interpretations in the most respected commentaries to let the text speak for itself, and as he listened with a passionate hunger and thirst for a word from God that would speak to his need and to the need of his time, what he heard shook his world like an earthquake. Instead of validating the established order it set a question mark against church and society alike and particularly against the church's preaching and practice, but at the same time it generated a vision of a new age. The Reformers are sometimes represented as innovators, founders of new churches, but that was not their intention. Their first concern was to restore the continuity of the church in its life and faith with the church of the Scriptures, with the Israel of the Old Testament and the New Israel of the New. They knew only one way to do it and that was by preaching and teaching from the Scriptures. John Calvin's influence in Geneva, and far beyond Geneva through Europe, flowed from those untiring interpretations of Scripture which sent him day after day into the pulpit of his Geneva church and which are preserved in his commentaries.

The Protestant Reformation was effected not by militant protesters and agitators but primarily by theologians and preachers who opened the Scriptures in such a way that men heard themselves addressed directly by a word from God that, in judging them and their world, liberated them from the past and, in offering them a new life in Christ, set them moving into a more promising future. What made Luther Luther was that one day the traditional interpretations of words and phrases in Paul's letter to the Romans began to fall away and with fresh ears Luther stood together with Paul, to a very large degree hearing what Paul heard and sharing the faith of Paul. Paul became the doorway through which Luther found access to the faith-tradition of the Scriptures and to the God of the Scriptures. A basic continuity was established with the line marked out by prophets and apostles and in the strength of that continuity Luther received his freedom to reinterpret. He had to come back through the doorway into his own time and, standing in the same faith-tradition or community of faith which he had found in the Scriptures, address the specific problems and situations of his own community as it faced the world of the sixteenth century.

The interpreter of Scripture has to live in two worlds. He has to be immersed in the world of the Scriptures with such intensity that at the heart of his being his most intimate companions are prophets, psalmists, apostles, and evangelists with Jesus Christ at their center. He lives with them. They are his first family, taking precedence over father, mother, wife, and children. He has to trouble to learn their language so that he may enter their world and listen with care to what they have to tell him. But he has also to be immersed in his own world, a man of his own time, open and sensitive to situations and dilemmas different from any that have ever existed before. Living in these two worlds at one and the same time, he becomes aware that they are not two worlds but one and the same world. The two worlds come together so that the Scriptures are like a magic glass through which we look to see ourselves, our fellowmen, and our world as they really are. We look *through* it in order to see ourselves and our own world. It is fatal when that transparency is missing. Far too often we look into the Bible and see only what is in the Bible. There are people who have studied the Bible with care for years and are thoroughly familiar with its contents but have never discovered themselves or their fellowman or their world in it, which is another way of saying that they have never seen past the words to the word of God. They remain prisoners of the words and concepts on the surface and have never become, like Paul and Luther, prisoners of the hidden word that makes them free, really free, for God's service in their own time.

There is no final formula, then, for making the Bible contemporary. There are only warnings against blind alleys and false approaches to the problem. There is no problem about the God of the Scriptures being contemporary. He is not just contemporary. He is always far out in advance of every age of man. The problem is not how to keep him abreast of us but how we may keep abreast of what he is doing in our world. The word of the Scriptures is the revelation of God's action not just in the past but also in the present and the future. The resurrection of Jesus revealed to his disciples that the truth and the divine reality that had met them and conquered them in him was not just an event of the past to be remembered but was also the power and wisdom of God with them in the present and the hope of their entire future. Let me repeat: there is no problem about the realities to which the Scriptures witness being contemporary. The problem is our obtuseness in binding them to the words and concepts of Biblical times, or of some one era in the history of the church, in such a way that they are not free to speak in their own way to a new and different day. In the last resort all that is needed is listening, that careful listening in which one's whole being and one's whole world is laid open to what is to be heard, and then the courage and integrity, no different in quality from the courage and integrity of prophets and apostles, to speak and act in faithfulness in the situations of our own time.

XIII

A Practical Postscript

IF IT IS TRUE that the Bible has very widely been falling silent in the church and has been fading from the consciousness of Christian people, we cannot be content merely to investigate the how and why of it and to discuss the prospect of a more adequate hermeneutic. Were we confronted with a deliberate attempt by some party to silence all or any part of the Scriptures, as Christians in Germany were during the Nazi era, 1933-1945, the analysis of the situation would lead to action. But here there are no such hostile forces to be confronted, only ourselves, the established order in our churches, homes, schools, and theological seminaries, the life-style of which we have become prisoners, the mental attitudes we have adopted unconsciously across the years, and, last but not least, our theology insofar as it provides for us a spiritual base that makes the Scriptures largely superfluous. If analysis is to lead to action, then the action has to be taken against ourselves and against the order in our institutions which we accept much too complacently.

Let us begin with the theological seminary. The twentieth century has been a time of remarkable progress in theological education. Fifty years ago the education offered in most of the seminaries on this continent was a very elementary affair. In some the classes were each conducted as recitations on the basis of a single textbook and students had no need of the library. In many the freedom of the scholar was subject to severe limitations. Most were training schools for preachers rather than centers of theological investigation. The change in the quality of the education in a half century has been profound. And nowhere has it been greater than in the Biblical departments. Even as recently as thirty years ago in some prominent seminaries professors of Old and New Testament had to proceed with caution in their presentation of critical theories and one can understand the atmosphere of timidity and uncertainty that surrounded the Bible for their students. But that day fortunately is past. Freedom to investigate the records of the past and to declare one's findings is almost everywhere an established right. But with the new day come new problems.

The more intensive development of theological scholarship and the higher intellectual standards has brought a greater degree of specialization. Each department of theology tends to develop in isolation from the others, engrossed in its own concerns, so that the student receives his education for the ministry in unrelated segments which he is left to put together himself as best he can. It is not uncommon to hear the complaint from him that he sees little or no relation between what he has received from the Biblical, the theological, and the practical departments respectively. Zeal for quality in each area of study can let the fact be lost from sight that the study is equipment for a ministry and that the fruits of it will be lost unless it is integrated with the other aspects of theology that are essential to the ministry. Theology as merely a specialized field of intellectual investigation is likely soon to drop away in the life of the pastor. Theology, however, is more likely to survive if it is a thorough facing of the critical question of how the church in its preaching and teaching, in its social and political action, in its total life, can be the faithful expression in the present-day world of that movement in history from beyond history which began with the prophets, Jesus, and the apostles. Perhaps if our seminaries were less conglomerates of specialized interests and more intimately communities of theological discussion, the student would discover more readily the interrelation of the various segments of his education and would be better prepared to continue that education beyond the seminary. What value have our higher intellectual standards if the theological activity begun in seminary is allowed to cease within three years of graduation, as some research suggests is frequently true? A pastor who has abandoned all serious theological study is not likely to deal very competently or confidently with the problems he has to face in letting the Scriptures recover their voice in the sophisticated world of today.

The two most serious criticisms that can be made of the usual curriculum in Bible are, first, that linguistic, textual, literary, and historical questions tend to occupy so much of the time that the theological content which is of paramount importance for the pastor receives minimal attention, and second, that students receive much more general introduction to the Testaments than specific training in exegesis, though exegesis should be for them a constant activity in preparation for preaching and teaching for the rest of their lives. Also, the methodology in exegesis is sometimes so thorough and elaborate in character that one would think they were being trained to write commentaries rather than to have a practicable method of exegesis in their daily use of the Bible in a parish. The parish situation should be envisaged constantly. It is not sufficient for a student to master a critical, historical, and theological approach for his own understanding of Scripture; he must have a grasp of it that will equip him to communicate that approach to his people. And it should be realized that the situation of the pastor with his people is much more difficult than that of the professor in a seminary with his class of students. The student must be trained not just to understand but to communicate his understanding to others.

Let us follow the graduate of seminary now into his first

parish or into whatever form of ministry he chooses. It is a critical point of transition. He goes from a situation in which he has the support and encouragement of professors and fellow students, and, not least, of a well-stocked library, to a situation where, once his fellow ministers have installed him, he finds himself very much alone. When he attends the district governing body to which he belongs, its sessions are likely to be wholly occupied with church business and to have no time for discussion of such matters as Biblical interpretation or theological issues. If he is to survive theologically, he usually has to do it on his own without companionship except from his books. It is not surprising that for many pastors the theological interest fails to survive, with serious consequences for the character of their ministry, but it *is* surprising that church courts fail to recognize that they have been neglecting what should be the first business of the church. The years of training in seminary are thrown away unless the community of theological discourse known in the seminary leads into a community of theological discourse and fellowship in the church. Certainly it should be a concern of every church court to counteract the forces that are robbing the Scriptures of their authentic voice.

From the church court we move to the local congregation and we ask why there is so rarely a willingness of adult church members to spend time in studying the Bible together. The young man mentioned in the preface could have knocked on the doors of many churches, large and small, far beyond the big city, with the same disheartening result, embarrassing all of them to confess that nowhere in their structure was there a class, comparable in quality to secular classes in adult education, for the exploration of the Scriptures. And, even where such a class is made available, not more than 5 percent of the members of the church are likely to make use of it. Ninety-five percent feel no need of it. Their version of the Christian faith and the Christian life is of a character that they can dispense with any serious delving into the Scriptures. They are content with a church in which all things are done decently and in order, which makes minimal demands upon their time and provides a maximum of moral stability and spiritual security for them and for the immediate community in which they live. It is significant that most of the office-bearers who provide the leadership and determine the policy of the congregation are usually among the 95 percent. It does not occur to them to ask what likelihood there is of them preserving a true perspective concerning the gospel and the church if they are indifferent to their continuity with the church of the Scriptures. They are too confident of their ability to remain faithful to Jesus Christ while ignorant of the Scriptures that witness to him.

But let no one, and certainly no pastor, underestimate the possible impact upon the life of a congregation when 5 percent of the membership begin to let themselves be laid open to the full range of divine and human reality that meets them in the Scriptures. Jeremiah described from personal experience the effect of confrontation with the word of God when he spoke of its power "to root up, to pull down, to build, and to plant." Let the ears be opened to hear what God has to say concerning man and his world and a ferment begins that can little by little change the whole structure of a church and of life far beyond the church. Ministers who are too busy to find time for such a study group have forgotten that the foundations of the church were laid not in large preaching situations but in a group of twelve. Also they might find in such a group a profound enrichment of their own relationship with Scripture and the inspiration for many sermons. Perhaps the reluctance of many ministers to provide for such adult study and discussion is that the complexity of modern Biblical scholarship overawes them. They are timid to expose themselves to the kind of questioning that such an intimate study group would invite. But, actually, all they need is the honesty to face their own and their members' questions one by one as they arise. By their training they have resources available to them that no one else possesses. They need only to be a few steps ahead of their people to be useful to them as their guide. What is required is not a minister who has all the answers but rather one who is willing to embark with his people upon a journey into the Scriptures which, if ventured with an unconditional openness, is likely to become a journey into an unknown future, an unfolding of new possibilities of human existence and Christian discipleship.

One would expect the church school to have some effectiveness in introducing children and young people to the contents of the Bible. But the Bible is not exactly a children's book and the attempts to make it one can succeed in making it a book that is left behind with childhood. Add to that the fact that teen-agers today desert the church school at about the age when they might begin a more constructive and interesting stage in their religious education. Take into account also the origin of many teachers in a precritical, pietistic, and highly individualistic orientation to the Bible, and the brevity of the time in which the education of youth is expected to take place, and all in all, it is not surprising that the church school has more often contributed to the silencing of the Scriptures than to a genuine understanding of them. Attempts at revolution in the church school are defeated consistently by the fact that it exists in the context of an adult congregation that considers an intimate knowledge of the Scriptures unessential in what it takes to be the Christian life. Yet the patient training of teachers is one of the most consistently fruitful and rewarding expenditures of a pastor's time and could be a major factor in the church's rediscovery of the Bible.

The achievements of some private schools in providing competent instruction in the Bible and stirring real interest in their students suggest one resource that might be much more widely exploited. The Supreme Court has already indicated that the principle of the separation of church and state by no means forbids the study of the Bible in the curriculum of the public school. Perhaps the time may come, with the improvement of relations between Catholic and Protestant churches and between Protestant denominations, and with the more general acceptance of a historical approach to Scripture, when it will be taken for granted that a knowledge of the Biblical literature is an essential part of the education that is offered by the public school. After all, why should Wordsworth or Walt Whitman or Ralph Waldo Emerson be permitted access to our children and Jeremiah and Jesus be forbidden to speak to them? It is ironic that it is usually those Christians who shout most loudly about the importance of the Bible who resist its introduction into the public school curriculum. The school should acquaint its students with a balanced picture of the history and the cultural forces that have shaped their world. To leave out the story of Israel or the story of Christianity is to falsify the picture of the past in which they have their roots.

The keyman, however, in all these situations is the pastor and preacher. It is from his sermons that the widest range of people get their taste of what the Bible really is about. He can so use the Bible that it serves to reinforce the complacent religious attitudes that freeze the church in a respectable ineffectiveness, or he can let it come open in such a way that its words are like charges of dynamite that blast the ice loose and set the stream in motion. He can have a preaching ministry that proceeds in isolation from the total educational program of the church or he can integrate the two and, by his open sharing of all he knows with those who are ready for such sharing, create a core of educational leadership for the future. He can in cooperation with other pastors and priests explore the possibility of some provision being made for education in the Bible in the public school. And perhaps if he were more vocal about the points at which his seminary training in the Bible failed to prepare him for his daily situation as mediator between the resources of the Scriptures and the actual situations of life in the community, it would speed the necessary changes in the seminary.

Finally, since throughout this book we have been emphasizing the complexity of the task of understanding the Scriptures and interpreting them to others, we may need to say what everyone who has read any distance into the Scriptures already knows: the prophets and apostles do not wait until we have perfected our hermeneutic before they begin to speak to us. They minister judgment and mercy to thousands every day who do not as yet even know that there is a hermeneutical problem. No one goes searching earnestly in their writings for a word that speaks to his situation without receiving his reward. Luther and Calvin were quite innocent of the enlightenment that more recently has been provided by historical criticism and yet they were able to let the Scriptures speak with life- and community-transforming power in their day. And today it is quite possible that a preacher with an atrocious hermeneutic who really cares what is happening in the lives of his people may let Scripture have its voice while another who is more concerned about the intellectual respectability of his discourse than about the coming of God into the midst of his people's life may produce only a silence. But that recognition of the power of God to speak through Scripture no matter how badly we interpret it does not thereby justify an irresponsibility on our part in the work of interpretation. The interpretative problem remains crucial to the life of the church and the history of our century makes plain to us that to ignore it any longer is to invite disaster.

Notes

Notes

1. Bultmann claims that he is not denying canonicity to the Old Testament and that to separate it from the New would be disastrous, but the assertion that the Old Testament is not revelation for Christians is surely tantamount theologically to a denial of canonicity.

2. Walther Zimmerli, *The Law and the Prophets: A Study of the Meaning of the Old Testament* (Harper & Row, Publishers, Inc., 1967), p. 2.

3. The theologian Friedrich Gogarten, who had been closely associated with Karl Barth and Rudolf Bultmann in the early twenties, found it possible to go along with the German Christians for a time, but it takes sharp eyes to detect in his theological writings of that time the deviation by which he laid a basis for his compromise. It is found in his doctrine of orders of creation, by which he provided a theological justification for nationalism. Emanuel Hirsch, who was a passionate nationalist and equally passionate in his rejection of the Old Testament, could in the very years of Nazism publish a book on the Christian faith that seemed to most readers to contain essentially liberal evangelical doctrine.

4. Otto Eissfeldt, *Kleine Schriften*, Vol. 1, p. 77. In an essay on the relation between Luther's hymn "Ein feste Burg" and Psalm 46, Eissfeldt says of Luther: "With the intuition of genius he recognized something unique in the

psalm and expressed it in his hymn, something which scholarly exegesis discovered only centuries later. This illustration makes clear to us that in the understanding of the religious documents of the past the historical critical exegesis of the scholar needs to have alongside it the experience-guided empathy of the herald of religion, that is, of the poet and preacher." Ernst Fuchs, more than anyone else, has emphasized in his writings that, since the Word of Scripture had its full reality in its original situation only when it was preached and heard, it recovers that reality today only when once more it is preached.

5. Schleiermacher's *Hermeneutik* early in the nineteenth century and Dilthey's works in the later years are best known and retain their value, but there were many other volumes from differing points of view.

6. Books such as J. E. McFadyen's *Guide to the Understanding of the Old Testament* (London: James Clarke & Co., 1927) were chiefly concerned to show how much more interesting and delightful the Scriptures were when historical and literary scholarship was permitted to make the text more intelligible. It was taken for granted that with such help the message of the Scriptures would be heard with new distinctness. No serious theological problem seems to have been anticipated.

7. Henry Preserved Smith, *Essays in Biblical Interpretation* (Marshall Jones Company, 1921). This history of interpretation mirrors the general consensus of scholars of that era that interpretation was now an established science and no longer a problem.

8. The fact that the concern of both Barth and Bultmann was focused upon the restoration to preaching of its original evangelical content and power naturally exerted an influence upon a wide range of scholars and has shaped the character of several series of commentaries in German, which aim to make the resources of both historical and theological interpretation available to ministers and laymen. Such commen-

taries, however, do not necessarily reflect the theology of either Barth or Bultmann.

9. Gerhard Ebeling, *The Word of God and Tradition* (London: William Collins Sons & Co., Ltd., 1968), pp. 11-31.

10. James M. Robinson and John B. Cobb, Jr. (eds.), *The New Hermeneutic*, Vol. II of *New Frontiers in Theology* (Harper & Row, Publishers, Inc., 1964), p. 67.

11. Dietrich Ritschl, in *Memory and Hope* (The Macmillan Company, 1967), speaks of the recent developments in hermeneutics as having been singularly unproductive in commentaries and then later refers to the wealth of commentaries that have flowed from the new theological developments in Old Testament, apparently not recognizing that the hermeneutical development embraces both Testaments but has had a somewhat different character among Old Testament scholars than among the post-Bultmannians. It is essential that the narrowing of the scope of the term "hermeneutics" be resisted.

12. Morton Smith, "The Present State of Old Testament Studies," *Journal of Biblical Literature*, March, 1969, pp. 19 ff., makes a slashing attack on what he terms "pseudorthodoxy," in which he lumps together those who use archaeology in the attempt to prove that the patriarchal stories are "true" and those who find in the Biblical text a witness to truth and therefore a theological content that still has relevance in the modern world. His valid criticism of conservative compromises in scholarly investigation is weakened by his own intemperate and blind refusal to recognize in Scripture a theological content that requires investigation and interpretation.

13. Adolf von Harnack spoke for many of his colleagues when in 1923 he denounced the new development of theology represented by Barth and Bultmann as an abandonment of scientific methodology that would undermine the position of theology in the German universities. The contributions of

both Harnack and Barth to the exchange of views are found in Karl Barth, *Theologische Fragen und Antworten* (Zollikon: Evangelischer Verlag, 1957).

14. Rudolf Bultmann, "The Problem of a Theological Exegesis of the New Testament," *Zwischen den Zeiten*, 1925 pp. 334 ff. Reprinted in Jürgen Moltmann, *Anfänge der dialektischen Theologie*, Vol II.

15. Rudolf Kittel, "The Future of Old Testament Science," *Zeitschrift für die Alttestamentliche Wissenschaft*, XXXIX (1921), pp. 84 ff.

16. Bultmann, *loc. cit.* See also his "The Problem of Hermeneutics," in his *Essays, Philosophical and Theological* (The Macmillan Company, 1955).

17. James M. Robinson follows this pattern in his sketch of "Hermeneutic Since Barth," in Robinson and Cobb (eds.), *op. cit.*, pp. 1-71.

18. For a more extended comparison of the hermeneutics of these two men, see my *The Divided Mind in Modern Theology: Karl Barth and Rudolf Bultmann, 1908-1933* (The Westminster Press, 1967).

19. Paul Tillich, *The Protestant Era* (The University of Chicago Press, 1948), p. xi: "There are objects for which the so-called 'objective' approach is the least objective of all, because it is based on a misunderstanding of the nature of its object. This is especially true of religion. Unconcerned detachment in matters of religion (if it is more than a methodological self-restriction) implies an a priori rejection of the religious demand to be ultimately concerned. It denies the object which it is supposed to approach 'objectively.'" Bernard E. Meland, "Theology and the Historian of Religion," *Journal of Religion*, 1962, p. 271: "I have been convinced for some time that modern scholarship has deceived itself in its strenuous effort to achieve purely objective inquiry. There is really no such thing as *purely* objective inquiry, that is, inquiry in which the interested, centered existence of the inquirer plays no part. At best there is a

disciplined use of our powers in which the bias of interest and conditioning are brought reasonably under control."

20. Wilhelm Pauck, in *Harnack and Troeltsch: Two Historical Theologians* (Oxford University Press, Inc., 1968), p. 19, quotes Harnack as saying, "There is no doubt that, with respect to the past, the historian assumes the royal function of a judge, for in order to decide what of the past shall continue to be in effect and what must be done away with or transformed, the historian must judge like a king." Pauck fails to see that here the historian fails to be humbled by any consciousness of his own historicity and subjects the past to himself in a way that silences its voice at many points.

21. On the inside cover of the *Journal* of the Evangelical Theological Society there is a statement of the "Doctrinal Basis" of the society: "The Bible alone, and the Bible in its entirety, is the Word of God written, and therefore inerrant in the autographs." This one doctrine, isolated from all others, is singularly unevangelical.

22. Otto Baab, *Theology of the Old Testament* (Abingdon Press, 1949).

23. James Barr, *The Semantics of Biblical Language* (Oxford University Press, Inc., 1961).

24. Hermann Diem, in his *Dogmatik: Ihr Weg zwischen Historismus und Existenzialismus* (Munich: Chr. Kaiser Verlag, 1955), in the English translation, *Dogmatics* (The Westminster Press, 1960), and in a smaller booklet, *Grundfragen der biblischen Hermeneutik* (Munich: Chr. Kaiser Verlag, 1950), has made valuable contributions to the debate on hermeneutics. Gerhard Ebeling, in his close association with Ernst Fuchs, makes hermeneutics as much the concern of dogmatics as of Biblical scholarship. H. G. Gadamer, *Wahrheit und Methode* (Tübingen: J. C. B. Mohr, 1960), brings the resources of philosophy to the discussion. More recently, Friedrich Mildenberger in two books, *Die halbe Wahrheit oder die ganze Schrift* (Munich: Chr. Kaiser Ver-

lag, 1967) and *Gottes Tat im Wort* (Gütersloh, 1964), has attempted to clarify the issues in hermeneutics by exploring the neglected wisdom of the dogmatic tradition. It is a source of weakness and loss in the English-speaking world that so rarely does a systematic theologian give his attention to the theological presuppositions of Biblical scholarship. A notable exception is the article by Langdon Gilkey cited in note 71.

25. The term "Biblical theology" created the illusion in many minds that the theological interest among Biblical scholars had brought into being a school of "Biblical theologians" among whom there existed a basic theological unity. The unity had about as much substance to it as there was among so-called "neo-orthodox" theologians, a term that at one time was thought to embrace a spectrum of theologians that included the two Niebuhrs, Tillich, Barth, Brunner, Bultmann, and others equally disparate. There has never been any basic unity among "Biblical theologians." Already, in the early twenties, Barth and Bultmann were pointed in quite different directions theologically, as I have shown in my *The Divided Mind in Modern Theology*. The post-Bultmannians today represent one distinctive stream of development, Cullmann and the enthusiasts for *Heilsgeschichte* another, the "purely descriptive historical science" school of Stendahl yet another, John Knox with his Christologically-centered, Anglican-process theology a fourth, and an assortment of scholars to some degree under the influence of Barth a fifth. The variations among Old Testament scholars are less broad but nevertheless are sharp. It is little wonder, therefore, that Biblical scholarship should seem to outsiders to be in a state of serious confusion. But the present disarray is more hopeful than the seemingly impressive unity of 1920. It is the consequence of new doors having opened up in the interpretation of Scripture, and it is not surprising that explorers in the new areas do not all move in the same direction or come back with the same report.

26. Krister Stendahl, "Biblical Theology, Contemporary,"

The Interpreter's Dictionary of the Bible, Vol. 1, pp. 418-432.

27. Wilhelm Vischer, *The Witness of the Old Testament to Christ,* tr. by A. B. Crabtree (London: Lutterworth Press, 1949).

28. Jerry Wayne Brown, *The Rise of Biblical Criticism in America: 1800-1870* (Wesleyan University Press, 1969), documents an earlier importation of German critical scholarship that failed, however, to take root.

29. In fairness, it must be recognized that the dominance of this viewpoint in the Society of Biblical Literature is in part the result, not of an absence of interest in the theological aspects of Biblical study, but of a fear that the raising of theological issues will be injurious to the cooperation of Christian and Jewish scholars. But surely it would be more in keeping with the service of the God of the Scriptures if Christian and Jew would look together at this deeper and more essential level in Scripture and discover that they are bound to each other not just by their common interest in ancient literature and history but by their very real common participation, each in his own way, in the stream of faith and life that flows from the Scriptures into the maelstrom of our world today.

30. It is significant that The Anchor Bible makes no provision for the exposition of the theological content of the text, but some authors have disregarded their instructions and produced theological commentaries rather than merely translations with notes.

31. A similar criticism may be made of Bultmann, who, as Norman J. Young, *History and Existential Theology* (The Westminster Press, 1969), has shown so clearly, makes a sharp division between two levels in history—the outer, factual level, which is accessible to historians (the *historische*), and the inner, personal, existential level, accessible only to faith (the *geschichtliche*). Only the second has theological significance. Barth sees these two levels as intimately related.

His separation of the two seems more practical than theological.

32. See the chapter on "Typology, Allegory, and Analogy," in my *The Interpretation of Scripture* (The Westminster Press, 1961), pp. 93-133.

33. It is significant that the hermeneutical discussion that has been so vigorous among the post-Bultmannians has produced so little in the way of commentaries. Exegesis is the acid test of any methodology. The Old Testament development has been highly productive in commentaries in Europe.

34. Albert Schweitzer, *The Quest of the Historical Jesus*, tr. by W. Montgomery (London: A. & C. Black, Ltd., 1910).

35. Credit for liberating Biblical theology from systematic theology is usually assigned to J. S. Semler. By 1800 the principle was well established.

36. See the fuller discussion of this in Chapter X.

37. It is Bultmann, and in succession to him Ernst Käsemann, who has been most ruthless in insisting upon this responsibility of critical scholarship, Rudolf Bultmann, *Glauben und Verstehen*, Vol. 1 (Tübingen: J. C. B. Mohr, 1954), p. 2, expresses his gratitude to liberal theology for imparting to him a sense of the necessity for a radical integrity in theological scholarship.

38. George Eliot, *Miscellaneous Essays* (Doubleday, Page and Co., 1901), pp. 105 ff.

39. Harry Overstreet, *The Mature Mind* (W. W. Norton & Company, Inc., 1949).

40. C. H. Dodd, *The Authority of the Bible* (London: James Nisbet & Co., Ltd., 1928). Reprinted for wide circulation in paperback, 1952.

41. C. H. Dodd, *The Bible Today* (London: Cambridge University Press, 1946).

42. John Bright, *The Authority of the Old Testament* (Abingdon Press, 1967).

43. Stendahl, "Biblical Theology, Contemporary," *The Interpreter's Dictionary of the Bible*, Vol. 1, pp. 418 f.

44. Bright, *op. cit.*, p. 63.

45. *Ibid.*

46. Vischer, *op. cit.*

47. Bright, *op. cit.*, p. 88.

48. *Ibid.*, p. 120.

49. *Ibid.*, p. 125.

50. *Ibid.*, p. 152.

51. *Ibid.*, p. 148.

52. Isaiah 42: 1-7; 49: 1-6. See the comment on these passages in my *History and Theology in Second Isaiah: A Commentary on Isaiah 35, 40-66* (The Westminster Press, 1965).

53. Bultmann meets this problem by drawing a line between an outer history—the events of world history accessible to the objective assessment of the historian—and an inner personal existential history, which is known only as one lets himself be confronted by it in the present. God is known only in this inner history, and there only as he is reflected in the changes in man's self-understanding. This must be seen, therefore, as a new form of historical methodology by which the scholar establishes a way of access to the ultimate content of Scripture. James M. Robinson, in his *A New Quest for the Historical Jesus* (Alec R. Allenson, Inc., 1959), understands Bultmann in this way and seeks to exploit this new way of access to the person of Jesus Christ. The God-end of the personal relation may be hidden, but at the man-end the way is open. God is a mystery, but not man! Walter Schmithals, "Barth, Bultmann, und wir. Zum Methodenproblem in der Theologie," *Evangelischer Kommentar*, Aug., 1969, pp. 417 ff., considers Bultmann's greatest achievement to be the devising of a historical hermeneutic or methodology that unearths the full content of Scripture and states it in the language of today, doing in a manner appropriate to our time what dogmatics used to do with its antiquated methodology. Such are the ambitions of the "New Hermeneutic," but its exposition of the "ultimate content" is not yet too

convincing. There may yet be a future for systematic theology!

54. James Barr, *Old and New in Interpretation* (Harper & Row, Publishers, Inc., 1966). Barr's tendency to overdrawn negativity, combined with a weakness in positive construction, mars his book and leaves the way into the future very vague. He has performed a valuable service, however, in his thorough critique of G. Ernest Wright's identification of revelation with acts of God in history from which Israel is said to have "inferred" its own election as a people of God and even the attributes of its God.

55. G. Ernest Wright, *God Who Acts: Biblical Theology as Recital* (Henry Regnery Company, 1952). Wright has restated his position in *The Old Testament and Theology* (Harper & Row, Publishers, Inc., 1969), but without making it more convincing and without taking any adequate account of the serious criticisms of it by Barr, Gilkey, and others.

56. Oscar Cullmann, *Salvation in History* (Harper & Row, Publishers, Inc., 1967).

57. Wolfhart Pannenberg (ed.), *Offenbarung als Geschichte* (Göttingen: Vandenhoeck & Ruprecht, 1961).

58. Richard Reinhold Niebuhr, *Resurrection and· Historical Reason* (Charles Scribner's Sons, 1957).

59. These terms are frequently confused by English and American scholars. The clearest definition of them is to be found in Norman J. Young's *History and Existential Theology*, pp. 22 ff.

60. Karl Barth, *Church Dogmatics*, Vol. I, Part 2, tr. by G. T. Thomson and Harold Knight, ed. by G. W. Bromiley and T. F. Torrance (Edinburgh: T. & T. Clark, 1956), pp. 492 ff.

61. Maurice Goguel, *The Birth of Christianity* (London: George & Allen Unwin, Ltd., 1953).

62. Karl Barth, *Die protestantische Theologie im 19. Jahrhundert: Ihre Vorgeschichte und ihre Geschichte* (Zollikon: Evangelischer Verlag, 1952); translated in part as *Protestant*

Thought: From Rousseau to Ritschl (Harper & Brothers, 1959).

63. Paul Hazard, *The European Mind: The Critical Years (1680-1715)* (London: Hollis & Carter, 1953), p. xv.

64. John Henry Randall, *The Making of the Modern Mind* (Houghton Mifflin Company, 1926).

65. *Heilsgeschichte,* or salvation history, is a concept developed, from yet more remote antecedents, by conservative theologians such as von Hofmann and Beck in mid-nineteenth-century Germany as they attempted to find room for the Biblical account of God's action in history in the vast expanse of world history that was then coming into view. It took various forms both then and later and is differently represented by such modern spokesmen for it as Oscar Cullmann, Ethelbert Stauffer, and A. G. Hebert.

66. Cullmann, *op. cit.*

67. I am indebted to Friedrich Mildenberger's *Die halbe Wahrheit oder die ganze Schrift: Zum Streit zwischen Bibelglauben und historischer Kritik* for pointing out the significance of this revolution in historical perspective. His whole book is a valuable contribution to the hermeneutical discussion. As a systematic theologian, earlier trained in Old Testament, he inquires what contribution the dogmatic tradition of the church can make to the clarification of present issues.

68. Rudolf Bultmann, "New Testament and Mythology," translated into English in Hans Werner Bartsch (ed.), *Kerygma and Myth* (Harper Torchbooks, 1961), pp. 1-44.

69. Bartsch has edited six volumes of essays on the subject in *Kerygma und Mythos,* Vols. I-VI. A bibliography of the literature is found in the English translation of Vol. I.

70. These two "worlds" correspond to the two ages in the theology of Paul, the world of sin and death which has been conquered by Christ but from which the Christian in this life is never wholly liberated and the new world inaugurated by Christ in which the Christian finds himself

to be a new man—truly human, truly fulfilled.

71. Langdon B. Gilkey, "Cosmology, Ontology and the Travail of Biblical Language," *Journal of Religion,* Vol. XLI (1961), pp. 194 ff.

72. Gordon D. Kaufman, "On the Meaning of 'Act of God,'" *Harvard Theological Review,* 1968, pp. 175 ff.

73. J. H. Bernard, *The Gospel According to St. John,* Vol. I (Edinburgh: T. & T. Clark, 1928), p. 21.

74. Robinson and Cobb (eds.), *op. cit.,* p. 34.

75. Rudolf Bultmann, *Existence and Faith* (Meridian Books, Inc., 1960), pp. 171 ff.

76. This chapter was added as a consequence of conversations with Prof. Ronald Wallace, of Columbia Seminary in Decatur, Georgia, which convinced me that in the original four lectures on "Hermeneutics and Homiletics," I had dealt inadequately with the necessity of the *text* of Scripture to a contemporary hearing of the word of God.

77. See a discussion of this in my commentary on Isaiah 35, 40-66, *History and Theology in Second Isaiah,* pp. 295 ff.

78. William Wrede, *Paul,* published in German in 1906; English translation published by American Theological Library Association, 1962.

John Henry Randall. <u>The Making</u> of <u>the Modern Mind</u>